# Sociology of Love

**Gennaro Iorio**

VERNON PRESS

*www.vernonpress.com*

Vernon Press is an imprint of Vernon Art & Science Inc.

*In the Americas:*
Vernon Press
1000 N West Street,
Suite 1200, Wilmington,
Delaware 19801
United States

*In the rest of the world:*
Vernon Press
C/Sancti Espiritu 17,
Malaga, 29006
Spain

Library of Congress Control Number: 2014935524

ISBN 978-1-62273-157-2

# Contents

# Preface

An initial research into a fundamental idea of social life is a complex job that is difficult to represent. Such diversity is particularly expressed in regards to love which is analyzed according to a plurality of styles and methods. Poetry, songs, psalms, romance books, biological and medical treatises, cultural inquiry, philosophical and theological analyses and practical manuals are all relevant for an understanding of the theme of love. Let us immediately state that this essay does not intend to review all of this literature, but will rather address a specific aspect; that is, the expressions of agapic love. It will not only be specific then, but it will consider at the sociological aspect of agapic love. This work will have two goals: the first will look at the conceptual definition of *agape*, while the second will try to make the concept operational for an interpretation of sociality at a micro level, of face-to-face relationships. It will attempt to so at the macro level as well: for historical processes lasting for long periods, yet without refuting the middle level, that is, for individual cases or actions interpretable by using the concept of *agape*. The more general aim is to introduce a new concept into the sociological lexicon, not out of an ideological spirit, but starting from the awareness that a sociality exists, made of people, relationships and actions, which the available tools of interpretation cannot render legible in its empirical manifestation. There is a seen but not recognized sociological interpretation, which impoverishes its very imagination. As Pierre Bourdieu had felt in the anthropological part of his work, there is a specific logic in the world of social interaction that is anchored to the logic of praxis. Such a dimension allows us to hypothesize that *agape* is known insofar as 'practical knowledge,' before being built by interpretative categories (Bourdieu, 1972/1983). This argument poses a problem for the statute of the concept of *agape* which regards actions done by individuals in the realm of reality and is therefore not an ideal, nor is it a utopia or a deception. Also Axel Honneth, in questioning the notion of *agape*, glimpsed an interest if we could find traces of it beyond people and communities socialized towards an agapic ideal (Iorio and Campello, 2013).

We are certainly not the first to use the concept of *agape* in sociology as, before anyone else, it was used authoritatively by Luc

Boltanski in the elaboration of his critical sociology. In particular, he uses the tool of political philosophy to remodel the cities associated with different forms of action, in order to delineate a regimen of peace-building actions in which tools offered by political philosophy are not very useful, therefore turning towards the tradition of Christian love, as studied only by theologians (Boltanski, 1990). That which we wish to reflect upon is not Christian sociology, since such a thing would be inconceivable and misleading for both dimensions of knowledge. We simply want to recognize the legitimacy in transferring a concept from a type of argument to another and, at the same time, the autonomy and the irreducibility of the one and the other. Hence, the objective remains the possibility of modelling empirically observable social action and not to offer a normative-ideal horizon to social action. This reflection is therefore closely connected to the historical situation and founded on the direct observation of reality, on the empirical data offered by experience, and will not be based om universal and abstract premises.

However, it would be interesting and useful to rethink the relationship between sociology and theology. This is because, if it be true that historically the social sciences in general and sociology in particular were born in order to free themselves from a certain dogmatic theology, it is also true that the course of sociological tradition and the relationship between the two disciplines has been in some cases very fruitful. One need only think of the concept of 'charism' introduced by Weber in sociological lexicon, taking up the work of theologians. Starting from this concept, the German sociologist developed his theory of power, distinguishing it as rational, traditional and charismatic. This is power founded on devotion, an uncommon obedience to the leader, justified by either a sacred characteristic or by the moral values of a person. Weber studied in depth the characteristics and the functions of the history of charismatic leaders, be it in the religious field as in the political one. Another famous case regards the concept of 'habitus' by Bourdieu, already delineated by the same Weber, and Elias. Medieval theological thought had developed the concept of supernatural 'habitus' (Lonergan, 1970) to bring to the fore that beyond the *gratia gratis data*, that is, divine grace given gratuitously, there is also the *gratia gratum faciens*, which expresses the necessity on the human's part to respond to the grace given. Such a concept of 'habitus' had been elaborated in antithesis to the lower-medieval idea of I cannot help sinning, that this, the impossibility of remaining on the 'straight path' without God's intervention, underlining here the responsibility on the part of the human being, his freedom, a fundamental premise to nascent modernity. Thomas Aquinas traced a middle road between the two positions and defined that the *gratum faciens* contains both an influx of God on the grace given, as well as the consequent actions of co-operative grace by humans. Therefore, the concept of 'habitus,' so essential to contemporary sociology, has its origins in its very relationship with theology, often forgotten and not explained by its very users. We retain that also *agape* can be included in this path full of pitfalls regarding the relationship between theology and sociology. We see above all, in this very historical moment, the need for a renewed relationship with social criticism. In fact, we maintain that *agape* is a critical concept of social reality and, for this reason, useful for comprehending and utilizing in the analysis of relationships between people. The 'sociology of critical ability' of Luc Boltanski and of Laurent Thevenot (1999) identifies the source of the criticism of society in the practice of subjects in their daily life, rather than in established abstract principles of a detached theorization. Boltanski introduces a distinction between reality and the world configured by regulatory and moral parameters, which show that every given 'reality' is always only one of the multiple realities possible. Since human beings are hermeneutical animals, they are always able to relate to a given reality in such a way that a gap can emerge between reality and the world. This is the place of criticism and Boltanski identifies two types: the 'reformist' and the 'radical' kind. Reformist criticism concerns those practices that turn out to be inadequate in respect to expectations and this is why they are criticized; radical criticism, instead, comes from the experiences of humiliating injustice which are not represented within the institutional framework of society.

In fact, in the current crisis it is important to develop a reflection on the concepts of social criticism and emancipation, in the awareness that the social dynamics taking place require a conscientious and reflexive response to the notion of criticism and a renewed attention to the conditions that allow for projects of collective emancipation that are empirically founded. As a mere introduction, we can bring to light two aspects which *agape* permits us to emphasize. The first concerns the relationship with the topic of emancipation. Given that criticism to ideological models typical of early modernity has been acquired, and starting from the need of avoiding every absolutism, this still leaves open the task for 'a criticism of reason through reasoning' and that of 'establishing perspectives through which the world is upset, remains strange to, reveals its fractures and its cracks' (Adorno, 1971/1951). Agape permits, on the one hand, this very affirmation and not an absolutism of cultural elaboration, and on the other, to reveal the contradictions, unacknowledgments and abuses. The second fundamental element of analysis could be made by the conceptual relationship with the social bond. Today, we are seeing a return to community, to a new need of belonging, a new need for roots. Alongside situations of a reactive type, such as new forms of religious, local, and ethnic community formation, etc. – there are however new forms of communities and of social bonds emerging – which attempt to build moments of social, but not exclusive, solidarity. Because *agape* is the most radical recognition of the single and the general, at the same time, it avoids every exclusion and any institutional form of violence by the exclusionists. At times it requires heroism, but more often, it is done through acts of daily living. There is no lack of examples from this point of view: new forms of social movements, of non-consumerist communities, of neighborhood associations and volunteerism, of collective participation, all bearers, in a more or less explicit and conscious way, of moments of social criticism and emancipation founded on actions which break with the logic of calculation and exploitation, so as to enter a practice of freely giving. A following reflection on the nature and the conditions of agapic love, in the current historical situation, appears then the best way to pose the question of criticism.

The book is divided into five chapters. In the first one, the definition of *agape* is outlined. Starting from the presentation of a recent sociological literature that rediscovers love in its diverse meanings, (and presenting a note on the theological root of the concept, but clarifying the scientific tradition of referral) we pass on to discuss Boltanski's perspective, who introduced the concept, in an incidental way, to express his sociology of action. After a criticism of this French sociologist, a definition of *agape* is formalized that finds its typical trait in the dimension of overabundance, to then exemplify five useful dimensions of agapic love in order to make the concept operational for its empirical use. Following this, we present six propositions of agapic love which are other dimensions of the concept and its ulterior semantic specifications. In the second chapter we will explain what is typical of this concept by bringing out the differences with other similar concepts: we will state what agapic love is not with respect to eros, philia, gift.Showing the need to introduce a new concept which has a heuristic foundation. The third chapter looks at love in the classics of sociology: Simmel, Weber and Sorokin are three classical sociologists who treated love with meanings that are close to agapic love, bringing out aspects useful to the economy of our substantive argument, but also for its empirical and historical-comparative aspects. Sorokin speaks of *agape* in sociology in an explicit manner, while Weber in a surprising way uses the concept of love in his comparative analysis of religion. Simmel offers numerous points to study agapic love and its social implications.

In the fourth chapter we look further into scientific literature, for authors and research which look at the dimension of agapic overabundance, even if they do not conceptualize the concept in agapic terms. In a micro dimension, we look at psychoanalytic post Freudian research by Winnicott, by the social theoretician Honneth and by the philosopher Marion, to show how love is the key for identity formation of the subject since his/her first moments of life; showing also how *agape* is tied to the dimension of struggle for existence. There is a macro dimension as well to *agape* that is useful for the interpretation of the origins of modernity, which takes the work by Szakolczai on the sociology of grace. Such a concept is expressed as *agape*, if we were to look at it from the point of view of the recipient of this social action. The fifth chapter looks at the middle empirical dimension, that is, there are three case studies: two individuals who, in tragic circumstances, in World War II and the ex-Yugoslavia, find the strength to act with agapic behavior capable of subverting the 'normality' of social interaction. They are those of Perlasca and Divjak; the third one, instead, examines the logic of a social movement that formed around the peer-to-peer software. All three cases exhibit the trait of overabundance and the absence of one's own intentions of an agapic behavior, nor do they have socialization to a faith as a premise to their own ethical parameters. However, without a concept of *agape* it would be impossible to bring out a dimension of a sense of an empirically founded social reality.

In the epilogue, we look at the critical capacity of the emancipative charge of *agape* on the cultural level.

Lastly, we must recognize that we are indebted to our friends who animate the experience of Social-One. The book is a fruit of different reflections, made on the topic of agapic love, which have been taking place for eight years already. My gratitude goes especially to

Vera Araujo, Rina Mulatero, Silvia Cataldi, Paolo De Maina, Michele Colasanto, Mauro Magatti, Arpad Szakolczai, Paolo Montesperelli, Raffaele Rauty and Filipe Campello. To all of these, I owe recognition for the continual greater understandings, stimuli and encouragements received.

Chapter 1

# What is agape

In the sixties, David Matza denounced the existence of the 'syndrome of Columbus' among the world's sociologists. He wanted to show that researchers often proposed new concepts that are not always useful in interpreting social reality (Matza, 1966), a tendency still alive today among scholars involved in this debate, each of whom, in their anxiety to interpret the new social configurations, propose conceptual novelties that are not always necessary to social analysis. The new concepts create a sense of frustration among scholars, in so much as they mine the necessary process of accumulation of knowledge that is typical of every scientific discipline. The objective of this chapter is to propose the concept of *agape* to social contemporary theory. It is ancient for theological research, and in many aspects, philosophical as well, but unprecedented for social sciences if not for more recent work such as Luc Boltanski's (2007). The effort to define the concept of *agape*, to trace its epistemological outlines so as to use it for empirical analysis, seems to us necessary to describe a social reality 'seen yet not recognized' by the conceptual apparatus used by current social sciences (Gouldner, 1997). Such an approach can be placed in the perspective of critical theory.

## 1.1 The Rediscovery of Love

Recently, sociology has rediscovered the concept of love, although researched in its meaning as that restricted to the dimension of eros and the sphere of couples. Doing some review on this topic, one can come across some great frameworks: the historical and at times diagnostic one by Sorokin; those of Elias, Giddens, Beck and Bauman; the one focused on sex as an exemplary case of interactive ritual by Randall Collins; and the one done to analyze the processes of commercialization of love by Arlie R. Hochschild, typical of a modernity characterized by calculation and quantification (Hochschild, 2003/2006). But there are other analyses on love, like those produced by Foucault on sexuality, seen as a form of experience. Such research has brought to the fore how individuals have been induced to recognize themselves as subjects of desire, as well as discovering in desire the truth of their being, first through an hermeneutical practice, and then through a disciplinary science, such as the biomedical and psycho-pathological one (1978).

According to Elias (1988), in the course of the process of civilization, intimacy is gradually confined to the private sphere in so far as it became an activity relegated to the behind the scenes. The bedroom, carefully hidden, becomes the lawful space for intimacy, while in public it generates embarrassment and shame. Since humanity no longer felt threatened by extinction, eros became separated from its biological justification and, as such, became a key element for constituting and continuing conjugal relations. Nowadays, eros has reached the point where we are seeing a further separation between conjugality and sexuality.

We point in merit to the contribution of Luhmann, for whom love corresponds to a peculiar communicative code. The communication convergence is, by definition, problematic, there being a contingency in the way in which a message emitted by Ego can be received by Alter. Given this multiplicity of possible meanings attributable to such an act, what would guarantee a semantic convergence? Here, Luhmann introduces the concept of code or symbolic medium, whose function it is to increase the disposition of the speakers to accept what is being said, selectively tightening the meaning of possible alternatives. Among these codes is love, in virtue of which the probability that a message put forward by Ego (as a request, prayer, offer, silence) be accepted by Alter, will be higher than its eventual refusal. Love works by convincing Alter of the goodness of the message put forth by Ego (Luhmann, 1987).

Giddens, instead, in his *The Transformation of Intimacy* (1995), rebuilds the passage from a marriage arranged on the basis of economic factors (therefore not a union bound by mutual attraction, but a family affair for the perpetuation of progeny and the conservation of patrimony) to the birth of romantic love.

The ideals of romantic love, spread by the first mass literary genre, the romance, meant as courtship, and the tale of an amorous relationship as a 'story,' represent one of the factors that liberated a marriage union from a relationship of convenience. From an immutable parental system that had been sent down through the generations, now, a way arises of establishing ties based on intimacy and sexuality. Romantic love, so to speak, takes the place of possessions and income in the search for a partner. Husbands and wives start to appear as partners in a common sentimental enterprise, which has precedence even over jobs and children. The home becomes an environment separated from work and, in contrast with the instrumental nature of this latter, coincides with the place for affection.

To this end, Giddens defines the concept of 'converging love,' or, rather, he presupposes the end of romantic ethos, which implies a strong asymmetry in the couple, and a contemporary domestic subjugation for the woman. What seems to be happening today is the possibility of a 'pure relationship,' characterized by sentimental, emotional and sexual equality between the partners, which is negotiable and worthy of continuation only if there are benefits therein for both, or if both retain it to be emotionally gratifying. The current 'divorcing society' is a demonstration and consequence thereof, when it indeed does not end in violence as many official statistics show (Giddens, 1995:59). It is on this last possibility – that of interrupting the relationship at any time – that Bauman's critical reflection is inserted (2004). In Liquid Modernity society, in which identity and lifestyle, as well as careers, must be constantly re-elaborated, emotional ties also become flexible. According to Bauman, although anxious to establish relationships, we are fearful of remaining trapped in stable relationships. Such anxiety is compensated for by turning to the principle of consumerist capriciousness: we do not build a relationship, yet a number of needs are satisfied. A symptom of this attitude is the obligation of staying perennially connected with a large crowd of people. The language of connection progressively substitutes that of relationship. And each connection is, by definition, a temporary one and therefore, substitutable: to disconnect is, in fact, a likewise legitimate choice. From Bauman's point of view, nothing is lasting, save for the speed of change: it would be this rhythm to redeem. Certainly, in late-modern societies, because of geographical mobility both for work and affection, the social circles to which we belong are multiple and varied, and our identity, as well as the social relationships we build, are not written in a compulsory destiny. From this brief exposition we can gather, firstly, that the topic of love is an object of study in recent sociological productions and it has been also for the reflection of authoritatively represented classics by Simmel, Weber, and Sorokin, whom we will speak about in the following chapter.

Finally, it is important to note how the sources, the empirical reference of a great part of the studies we cite, with the exception of

Elias and that of Giddens, Luhmann, Beck or Hochschild have lost the sense of the real person. In fact, they refer to tales, romances, as well as questions by readers to experts, tabloid papers, and internet announcements. People, and their actions, the meanings given to actions, and observations, disappear in a path of abstraction of representations of love: people are substituted by celebrities. We must, however, realize that love, the object of analysis, is rooted ever more, on the one hand, in the private life of people, losing social meaning or assuming a relevance only as indirect and secondary affection, while on the other hand, it is prevailingly understood in the sense of eros, as a couple, affectivity and emotionality. But if we partake in this new sociological observation of love as eros, which at times stammers on the sense of love as philia, it has generally remained silent on that of *agape.* However, there are other authors who have considered love as a force capable of generating social bonds, of transforming or reviving human relationships. It is a love that is rooted in the public actions of people, which pervades the living together of singles, of social groups and of communities; that is, agapic action.

Be it in traditional French criticism, as in the German one, a recent review of social criticism was begun starting from the concept of love. In Germany, the revision of critical theory has been done by Axel Honneth. We wish to discuss two aspects of the rich social philosophy of Honneth (2009). In first place, in his most recent writings, he underlines that love and respect – as well as rights – are necessary so that human beings may be able to live autonomously. This inter-subjective recognition is intended as a prerequisite for individual autonomy.

Secondly, Honneth sustains that the multiplication of spheres of recognition requires a more complex historic rebuilding than a mere referral to institutional realizations brought by the historically placed proceduralism of Habermas, who, from this point of view, puts distance between himself and his teacher (Honneth, 1992). For Honneth, normative theory should not build a neutral point of view from which principles of justice may be identified and extrapolated. Rather, it should rebuild those principles on the basis of historical processes of recognition in which they are already effective as rules for mutual respect and consideration. Significantly, Honneth sustains that such a theory can have 'trust in historical reality' because socialized subjects already have, as a guide, the principles that theory must only explicate. This move is an opportune and necessary historification of the debate on normative principles.

In France, the starting point is the 'sociology of critical ability' (1999) by Luc Boltanski and Laurant Thèvenot, who define in the subjects' daily practices, rather than in a detached theory, the source of social criticism. Boltanski introduces a new distinction between reality and the world, configured by moral and regulatory parameters, which show that every 'reality' presented is always only one of the many possible realities. Since human beings are ergonomic creatures, they are always capable of relating to a reality in such a way that a division between reality and the world may emerge. This is the place of criticism (1999). In *De la Justification*, Boltanski identifies two types of criticisms: the 'reformist' and the 'radical.' Reformist criticism concerns those inadequate practices in respect to expectations and are criticized for this very reason; radical criticism, instead, comes from experiences of injustice and humiliation which are not represented in society's institutional framework. In this context, Boltanski discusses the concept of *agape*, which we will consider more in depth shortly.

Briefly then, in a world without foundations, the root of criticism is offered by the historical ability of subjects immersed in their daily lives, of sharing a critical normative picture of reality. The space for criticism is given by the distance between 'reality' and the regulatory world possible but, at the same time, detected in historical procedures.

In the Italian context, we have noted a renewed interest in love, no only did two scientific reviews, that are, *Sociologia* (2011) and *Societa'. Mutamento e Politica* (2011) dedicates an exclusive issue to it, but also various scholars have analyzed this topic, pointing out the need to look at love for its social relevance. In this context, we are interested in highlighting the work of Pierpaolo Donati, according to whom love awaits for 'a conceptual patrimony that is not always available' (Donati, 2011a, p.170) and observes an inadequacy in the symbolism of eros, philia and *agape* in our differentiated societies (ibid., p.174) and therefore highlights the need for a new configuration of love.

In keeping with his relational sociology, he highlights that:

> "love, as seen as relationship, is the care of the Other. . .
> in as much as the subject in/of a relationship that oth-
> erwise would not exist without him/her." (ibid., p.177).

Further on, he underscores that love is a symbolic code of the latency that communicates to the other codes, (eros, *agape* and philia) how they should operate. Donati means to say that the constitutive need of a human being is to be in relationship, which offers the possibility to the different declinations of love to manifest themselves. The analysis by Donati appears to be truly interesting because it re-proposes the topic of love and highlights its social relevance. All the same, it appears reductive when it deals with the different forms of love, considering them as the difference generally of a type that is the latent metacode of relationships of caring, and, in addition, re-stricts love to care - thus recalling, in an implicit manner, the Homeric root of the verb *agapan*.

## 1.2 What Method of Research

Let's step back and explain what epistemological perspective we will assume in proposing a concept such as *agape*. The approach is typical of the social sciences tradition (Crespi et. Al., 2000; Honneth, 2002; Iorio, 2005). In fact, one cannot deny that modern social theory was born when the idea matured on the theoretical plane that the social order is not the product of virtues defined in the abstract, from which a good society alights for individuals but, unlike this prospective, society has been identified as the prevalent effect of practices and actions of a collectivity. In fact, the new, modern social theory represents a break with ancient classical theory which began from Aristotle until the natural law of Ugo Grozio, which includes also the Medieval Christian concept. Before being theoretical, the fracture had a methodological character, in so far as the social order was no longer been considered the product of an ethical principle of virtuous behavior, but the effect of concrete actions by subjects, even the irrational and unreflective ones. Therefore, the theoretical problem has become the observation and analysis of dominant activities and relationships.

Such innovation was accelerated by the social change that came about in late Medieval times and clarified during the Renaissance: the introduction of new commercial methods, the printing press and the formation of commercial cities were phenomenon no longer interpretable as the effect of the normative order of virtuous behavior (Sombart, 1902/1967). In this context, Niccolò Macchiavelli, in exile from his city of Florence, overturned all the anthropological premises of the philosophical Aristotelian tradition when he represented the human being as an egocentric individual, striving towards the pursuit of his own good, constantly driven by ambition, who faces every subject with an attitude of inevitable mistrust. The object of political science became the modality through which those retaining power could use conflicts arising among humankind to their own advantage.

After about a century, Thomas Hobbes, during the English Civil War, using research done by Galileo Galilei and the theory of knowledge by Decartes, chose the study of the laws of civil life as his objective by using the premises of the analysis of facts already established by Macchiavelli. Hobbes therefore brought to completion the anti-Aristotelian thought, according to which the essence of civil life is no longer virtue as lived among subjects but, inversely, subjects are considered in their normality to be estranged and impenetrable, projected at enlarging their individual potential for power with the aim of preventing aggression by others perceived as possible threats. For this reason, he introduced the contract as a tool to turn over to a Leviathan the powers of each person, thereby renouncing some freedoms in order to entrust the control of individual differences to the state.

Successively, Hegel emphasized that society is not born by an original contract, but took into consideration the hypothesis that relational and inter-subjective ties are at the basis of each socialization process and of relationships forming community (Hegel, 1971, pg. 127).

On the methodological plane today, there is another element to be recalled. Scientific knowledge cannot be thought of as an objective and neutral mirror of reality, as retained by positivists at sociology's beginnings (and of social sciences in general), but, to the contrary, it appears as a selective activity as regards a reality that seems to be ever more a continuous flow of events, whose meaning can only be found through concepts which render intelligible the apparent chaos which characterizes it. The lesson of Max Weber and his method of ideal types wants to in fact indicate a path to us and a way out of the impasse to which one may be led by a de-construction that denies the very possibility of a scientific analysis of reality (Weber, 1922/1958). Such an approach had to be made into a system not only by Emmanuel Kant, who had shown how knowledge was possible through some 'a priori' intellectuals – which permits us to perceive reality – but also by Friedrich Nietzsche, who affirmed that there are only interpretations of reality and not facts (Nietzsche,

1990). Scientists from physics and mathematical disciplines also arrived at these same conclusions: one need just remember the thermodynamic theory and Max Planck's quantum physics, Albert Einstein's theory of relativity, Niels Bohr's atomic theory, Heisenberg's uncertainty principle, Gödel's incompleteness quantum theorem (Crespi, 2002). According to these authors, knowledge comes through progressive approximations of concepts of reality. Every form of scientific knowledge is revealed to be partial and mediated by categories which permit us to define constants and connections between elements of reality. In this direction then, we may agree with Robert K. Merton when he recalled the process of serendipity, that is, of a journey of scientific knowledge along the inescapable axis between research in the field and theoretic elaboration (Merton, 1949/1959-1971).

An important contribution in recent social theorization is offered by analytical philosophy of language and by hermeneutics, which, starting from work by Jürgen Habermas has entered the scene as a new way to make the subject a protagonist in sociological interpretation. Even if in the symbolic inter-action of George H. Mead and in phenomenological sociology of Alfred Schütz, the symbolic order was central to the analysis of intentional social behavior, with Ludwig Wittgenstein, the social world is analyzed through linguistic actions, presupposing a correspondence between language and social order.

The meanings of words are not independent from concrete forms and from particular socio-cultural contexts; rather, reality becomes the product of interpretations connected to concrete living practices. Of particular usefulness in our analysis of *agape* is the hermeneutical approach developed by Georg Gadamer, who defined the hermeneutical circle through which knowledge is a dialogue between the interpreter and its subject who is always open to new possible intersections between 'request' and 'reply.' Under this perspective, language permits inter-subjective verification of understandings on meaning of things and events. Therefore, every understanding is interpretation and every interpretation is translation from different worlds and, for this very reason, language is the most authentic expression of every form of social experience. Linguistic perspective shelters sociological knowledge from every claim of objectivism and thoroughness, recognizing its very partial character as temporary and stipulative of every scientific conclusion.

Therefore, it offers as premise also to our analysis on *agape* the limits belonging to the epistemological statute of social sciences.

# 1.3 The Concept of Agape

Agape is an unknown concept for sociology, studied by Christian theologians to express that novelty indicated through a Greek word seldom used since the time of the Gospel writers: "God is love; and he who abides in love abides in God and God in him" (1 Jn 4:16). These words from the First letter of John express with singular clarity the core of Christian faith. For this reason John can say:

> "Beloved, let us love one another because love is of God; everyone who loves is begotten of God and has knowledge of God. The man without love has known nothing of God, for God is love" (1 Jn 4:7-8). "For this reason we can be sure that we love God's children when we love God and do what he has commanded" (1 Jn 5:2).

With the Christian message, love takes on a new centrality, characterized in second place by being a command and in first place by the universal dimension, meaning, by the coincidence of God and love (Mt 5:44; Lk 10:29 and, following, The Good Samaritan; 1 John 1,4,7 and following), which overturns the Hebrew and Hellenic conception and puts God as the object (and more precisely as only object: we do not love the other as such, but God in man and woman) and subject (God the Father) of love. Then even in Christian thought love reveals a close bond with death, since it is in death on the cross that love culminates and God and Agape realize their connection. Furthermore, with Paul's letters (1 Cor 13:7-13) *agape* becomes fundamental also as bond for the religious community. In Christian thought love reveals a close connection with the death, with the kenosis theologians say, that with the humiliation of God, since it is in death on the cross as a sacrifice of self for others, that you love expressed at its maximum intensity and Agape God and realize their coincidence. In addition, with the Letters of Paul (I Cor 13, 7-13) *agape* also became important as the bond of the religious community. Also for this aspect of the theologians coin a term: pericoresi to indicate that love has a social dimension and excludes any solipsism.

There were traces of love already in the pre-Christian era. Historical philosophy had, in contrast with the Aristotelian one, already emphasized the universality of love. In Christianity though, there begins an affirmation of a new type of relationship, that of agapic love, which is universal by its very nature, which urges one to love one's enemy as well (the non-friend, who may remain such even after having been loved) and which breaks the tendency towards selectivity which other expressions of love inevitably bring along with it. This new dimension of love was translated by the first Christians with the Greek word *agape*, which is almost a neologism, because it was present in ancient Greek as the verb *agapan*, but never as a noun that became indispensable to express a new way of loving that was non-describable through eros and philia alone (Coda, 1994).

The first Christian community chose a term from common Greek that was in disuse because they wished to express a novelty, a new experience of love which they had experienced as 'elimination of other alternatives.' In the Greek language there are at least five different words for the word 'love,' but only three of them appear in the New Testament: *agape* 258 times, 90%; *Phileo*, which is translated as affection, 31 times (9.9%); and *Thelo*, once. The Latins translated *agape* with *Charitas*, which indicates a connection between 'love and grace, gratuity.' Caritas, without the 'h,' instead indicates a lack of goods, or scarcity.

However, theologians highlight that the word *agape* is already found in the Old Testament, in the Canticle of Canticles, in the translation of the Bible from Hebrew to Greek of the Third Century B.C. in Alexandria of Egypt. The Greek translators, facing the various uses of the expression love, in translating the books of the Bible, betray a certain embarrassment. For a type of love, which in Hebrew is expressed with *dodim*, that of desire, the use of *eros* was fine, but for the other Hebrew term, *ahaba*, that is, spousal love made of *eros*, but also of mutual gift, the Seventy could not find anything better than the adoption of the word *agape*, chosen because of a certain harmonious sound, from the verb *agapao*, found already in Homer and meaning 'taking care of.' Its history is however very complex. Consider, for example, that in its single occurrence in the Canticle (5:1), dodim is translated (erroneously?) as adelphoi. In Proverbs (7:18) it is translated as philia, while in the same verse, ahava (plural) is translated as eros, while in Ezekiel dodim is translated twice with a participle of katalyo (Coda, 1994).

For the first Christians, *agape* indicated also the fraternal banquet one took part in during the Eucharistic Celebration. This ambiguity of *agape*, the love-banquet, expresses, more than any other theory, the novelty of this type of love that is a new form of life in common.

### 1.3.1 Boltanski's States of Peace

The starting point for our reflection on *agape* is the work of Luc Boltanski. He grasps and defines the various 'spheres of action,' which he subdivides into 'sphere of argument' and 'sphere of peace.' Boltanski highlights the existence of different contexts of action, each of which has elaborated its own *procedures of justification*, therefore, specific *rules* and *competences* through which the meaning of an action is built and its very identification, on the part of the agent and of the recipient. This theoretical element allows us to build a 'lay' approach to the topic of *agape*, seeing it as a possibility for social interaction which, on the one hand, does not exhaust the wealth of practical actions and of social types, yet, on the other, it is not excluded *a priori* as an impracticable and ideologically oriented action. Consequently, from the logical-theoretical point of view, *agape* is an action which can stand with dignity beside other possibilities of action (instrumental, expressive, functional and symbolic, etc.) In fact, perhaps it itself can traverse single subjects in different moments of their lives, and its exclusion from theoretical analysis up to today has surely been an ideological operation, which sociology has assumed responsibility (Boltanski, 2005). Within its effort to re-found a 'moral sociology' of Durkheimian tradition (the analysis of social action starting from subjects' ideal reasons), Boltanski shows that, in diverse contexts, the practices of justification of actions confer centrality to the subject, too often squashed by the dimension of social structure in sociological representations. This is one of Boltanski's general theoretical objectives: to re-evaluate the dimension of subject in respect to structure, privileged instead by his teacher, Bourdieu (1930-2002).

In a 'state of peace' people renounce utilitarian action based on exchange and act by giving more than what the situation requires. To analytically define this state of peace, Boltanski reasons on three forms of social ties built by love, as they have been traditionally described: the theory of Aristotelian love (*philia*), the Platonic one (*eros*) and the Christian (*agape*). The latter, for the French sociologist, being the state characterized by:

1) 'renunciation of equivalence': because the use of any measurement capable of counting that which has been given and received is annulled, as each is placed in the social relationship as irreplaceable, unique, singular;

2) 'neglect of the past and future': *agape* is concentrated on the present moment, the only anchor to acting without looking at what happened previously or could happen in the future. All is oblivion or ignorance and for this reason its temporal horizon has no limits. Such a dimension prefigures the third characteristic;

3) 'Absence of anticipation in the interaction': the person in an agapic state is silent, suspending every judgement of the interlocutor, and does not anticipate any action or conjecture, since he is entirely focused on the present moment;

4) 'Silence of desires': because *agape* acts while keeping in mind the other's needs, freely giving;

5) 'Practical action, realization': *agape* is, first of all, a social action, a process. It is not a sentiment, a state of feeling and intention. It looks at that which people have that is concrete and unique: '*agape*' – writes Boltanski – is activated only if is urged to come about by the presence of single individuals, but the people it turns towards are those it encounters on its journey and whose eyes it meets (ibid, pg. 75).

On this point, however, it is important to add that the action should be intended in a Weberian sense, that is, as an attitude which, besides doing something practical in regards to Alter, it understands also a 'not doing,' a 'letting go of,' or also an 'enduring' (Weber, 1999, pg. 4).

### 1.3.2 A Critical Note

This by Boltanski is, in our view, an important analytical reflection of the concept being examined, and the characters previously exposed are obviously of great value for the empirical analysis of 'Homo Agapicus.' It is also interesting to highlight how, besides the regime of justice with its reference to political philosophy, there is also a regime of peace, whose reference point can only be normatively theological. Correlated to this level of sharable analysis, there are other less convincing aspects. In fact, for Boltanski, *agape* cannot be transformed into a project; it cannot be posed as the objective of an action intentionally aiming to establish relations of love and, therefore, to producing adequate institutional forms. For this reason *agape* cannot be the object of: 1) discussion; 2) a theory; 3) a project: 3.1) neither personal, 3.2) nor social.

This is impossible for Boltanski because the use of the language would presuppose, in fact, that the actors have left *agape* and, therefore, have taken on that distance that allows one to consider, evaluate and describe from the outside the relationship of love. Such a negation is acceptable in the sense that *agape* does not speak of itself, since it is not auto-referential and has no need to justify itself. However, the idea that *agape* cannot make itself into discussion is criticizable in respect to three arguments, synthesizable then with the exclusion of the reflective dimension in Boltanski's *agape*, on the one hand, and in the absence of any contextual reference, of generating a new social content on the other.

Margaret Archer begins a recently written book with this, on how social action commences, indicating its driving force in the 'interior conversation': 'If we as human beings were not reflective, there could not exist anything similar to society. Whatever form of social interaction, from the dyad to the global system, presupposes that the subjects know, so to speak, to be themselves. If it were not so, they would not be able to recognize the words they say as their own, and neither would they be able to recognize the 'paternity' of their intentions, initiatives and reactions' (Archer, 2006, pg. 77).

a) Boltanski, in his work *L'Amour et la Justice comme competences* (1990), tries to distance himself from interpretative schemes that are too structural, typical of his teacher, Bourdieu, as shown previously. In pursuing such an objective, Boltanski adopts elements of the philosophy of language in his analytical framework, to signal the autonomy of the subject from the social structure. He takes into serious consideration the analyses of the rules of definition of competences and procedures of justification of social action, which take place specifically with the use of language. In the state of peace, instead, the characteristics of *agape* induce the subjects to do away with words, in contrast with its very initial theoretical intentions. In action founded on love for others, the element of subjectivity typical of people would be absent.

In fact, while not emphasizing language and its auto-referencing in the social building of reality, Wittgenstein (1889-1951) showed how the word is constitutive of social reality and how a lived experience, if it is unsaid, perhaps does not even exist. Such an intuition is taken up successively by Habermas in his theory '*Theory of Communicative Action*' (1981) to criticize, on the one hand, the reductionism which Marxist structuralism falls into and, on the other, to underline how the lives of people is characterized by language which allows society to reproduce through mutual understanding of the subjects living in it.

So, the language and the experience lived out by the process of the aware subject and communicated to his interlocutors is an important mechanism of reproduction of the social content in general, and therefore, also in agapic action. At the same time, language allows one to manifest the reflexivity and subjectivity of people which otherwise, as in the case of Boltanski, would be denied, with alienating and bureaucratic effects for the life of the subjects and their interactions.

b) Boltanski speaks of *agape* moving from a more general objective which concerns the re-foundation of a moral sociology, meaning, of action starting from one's ideal motivations. How is it possible to pursue such an objective, without considering from a general reflexive dimension of the individual his ideal motivations? This also includes the dimensions which characterize the individual, such as affection, will and cognitive ability, which regard his actions, the context of reference, his interlocutors, etc? Therefore, one should introduce the constructive dimension in Boltanski's framework of agapic action, otherwise one would fall into a logical contradiction with his very interpretative key. An example is the very life of Francis of Assisi, taken by Boltanski as a typical case and empirical source of *agape*. Francis suffered, reflected and practiced an ascetic climb while living *agape* in relation to others, the world, and himself. After, Boltanski paradoxically refers to the rule of St. Francis to indicate historical cases, while he is theorizing that the reflection on love makes one exit from love itself: but the written word is an even bigger distancing oneself from one's action than the spoken word. A second contradiction, this time between his theoretical framework and his reference to empirical reality, shows us the need for introducing the word in agapic action.

c) Agape is totally concentrated in the present moment, but for certain aspects every significant social action has this characteristic. Alfred Schutz has sustained a thesis by which I could not:

> "affirm with my reflection my own action while executing it, but I can affirm exclusively my completed

> action (my past action): ...to understand my behavior
> I must stop and think..." (Schutz, 1979, p.188).

Therefore, behavior is inevitably connected with a reflexive dimension by the same person, on pain of its negation. For this reason, the reflexive dimension of agapic behavior, as for any other human behavior, is essential and does not deny its peculiarity.

Finally, if we were to accept the traits of agapic action as defined by Boltanski, we would find ourselves paradoxically in a reality resembling more a world of nomads, of un-communicating robots, among whom *social* and *relational interaction* was abolished. There would only be action left, which is not social, because lacking its constitutive dimension of meaning. Boltanski states:

> "Balance would be achieved only by a 'letting be done'
> which would exclude even one's own theorization. In
> fact ... *agape* is not an inter-actionist model" (pg. 141).

In the 'state of peace' *social action* is excluded because it lacks intention gifted with meaning, there is no social interaction because everyone lives in the forgetfulness of the past and the future, deaf and indifferent to actions done by others, but committed only to giving. Social interaction is lacking because this action throws into oblivion any referral to a context in which the action is being done: he simply does not care! And yet, the only historical source used by Boltanski, St. Francis, was aware of the times in which he lived; he proposed to reform the Church, he exchanged ideas with St. Clare, he responded to the 'call of God' and dialogued to go deeper in the spiritual dimension of his life, etc.

In conclusion, we can say that Boltanski is an authoritative author who opens a new field of research, that of agapic action. In our intentions, however, the research path should start there where he left off: on becoming discussion, theory and project for oneself and for society, thereby recuperating a history that risks losing the subject, the concrete individual, in all of his constitutive dimensions.

# 1.4 Definition of agape

Our perspective defines *agape as an action, relationship, or social interaction in which subjects overabound (in giving, in receiving, in not giving or doing, in not taking care) of all its antecedents, and therefore, it offers more than the situation demands with the intent to bring benefits.* Hence, *agape* is defined starting from itself and for itself without interest, without a return, accountability or justification. Agape shows itself in its own process. Therefore, it is not a utilitarian action, or a market exchange, because no one offers or asks according to a calculated principle of marginal utilities for him/herself, nor is it founded on a principle of justice in giving or rendering according to a distribution criterion. It does not even appertain to the logic of solidarity which implies participation to a condition that does not belong to one, or of having the following or respect of others for our social status.

In general, in order for *agape* to be born, it does not even presuppose reciprocity, in as far as he who loves often finds himself breaking the cycle of having to give back: for example, it does not return a slap to the one who first gave it. In any case, in order to be activated, an agapic attitude does not start from the expectation that the other return the gesture. If there was necessarily a need for reciprocity, we could not interpret as agapic love all those empirical phenomenon in which a subject loves or has been loved by *anonymous* individuals: e.i. adoptions-at-a-distance, where a child is loved by people unknown to him. Furthermore, those situations of loving one's *enemy*, which by definition is the very one incapable of reciprocity since he does not care to return the love given to him, could not be interpreted. Yet *agape*, in its radicality, loves even the ungrateful type, that is, the one who does not wish to be loved, who does not want to render back the love given or who simply can't stand it: in this case as well he is a type characterized by absence of reciprocity. The anonymous, the hostile, the ungrateful are three types who do not annul *agape*; they do not undermine it since it is overabundance, in the sense of offering more than what the situation demands, so it can exist even without the return of reciprocity (Marion, [1997] 2001).

Therefore, in a Weberian sense, the typicality of *agape* is given by overabundance, that is, of giving more than the situation demands or more than what one has received according to a given measure; one has *agape* when individuals refuse to keep count and show unconditional behavior, unexplained by a criterion of *do ut des.*

# 1.5 Five dimensions of agape

In Sorokin's perspective there are five dimensions of love, which we now list, adapting them to our methodological viewpoint and to our own definition of *agape*. They are: 1) Intensity; 2) Extension; 3) Duration; 4) Purity; 5) Adequacy (Sorokin, 1954-2005, pp. 54-81). Agape can, then, vary in:

*Intensity:* This is minimal in the person who preaches *agape* but does not practice it; and it is null when it is used to mask selfish actions. Actions of love of low intensity are like offering a piece of bread to the homeless man or ceding one's place in line at the doctor's office. Actions of great intensity are, instead, all those gestures through which a person offers health, life, joy and advantages to others. Hence, there are multiple levels of intensity which overlap between the minimal and the maximal. This way, we can tell if a level is greater or less than another, what intensity is higher and which one is lower with respect to another. Consequently, we can establish a different intensity in the gesture of donating an organ to save another's life. Certainly, in this way, offering 2% of one's belongings has an inferior intensity to that of offering 50%. Dedicating an hour of time to others has an intensity inferior to the one dedicating four, five hours, or the better part of one's life.

*Extension*: Is a dimension that expresses the character of openness to the concept of good by the subject, the possibility of going towards doing everything for others and of accepting it as constitutive of one's owns actions. Between the minimum (love of self) and the maximum (love for the cosmos and for humanity), there are various intermediate levels such as, for example, love for one's family, for a few friends, or for all the groups to which one belongs. The maximum point is love for the entire human family, the universe, water, animals, the environment, etc. In this case, we can also put an ascending order to events and actions.

*Duration*: It can vary from the briefest of moments to the entire course of a person's or groups' life. A typical case is the person who dedicates his life to taking care of a sick person (such as a parent who assists a seriously handicapped child), or of an individual who offers a long period of financial help to a child through an adoption at a distance. These are all examples of long-lasting love. We can refer to actions of brief duration as those soldiers in a war who risk their lives so as not to kill the enemy and then in ordinary life return to other types of behavior.

*Purity*: It may present various gradations. It may go from a maximal level which finds its 'raison d'etre' in *agape* itself, to a minimal level characterized by love as a means to reach an interested outcome or that is part of a logic of equivalence, measure, and quantity between what has been given and what one has received. In this last case, the exiting from an agapic state is self evident.

*Adequacy*: This concerns the relationship between the subjective intention of *agape* and its objective manifestations, and it happens when the two dimensions coincide. However, the two dimensions can conflict. In this case we can have an inadequacy of love which can manifest itself according to two modalities. The first one concerns all those experiences of *agape* which can be subjectively authentic in the person who is doing the loving, but has objective consequences that are contrary to the intentions of that individual person. The second is characterized by a person who does not act subjectively according to agapic logic; he does not mean to love, but the consequences of his actions produce an objective benefit to other subjects and are, in fact, overabundant. For example, many creators of masterpieces such as Bach, Mozart, Beethoven, or Michelangelo were motivated in their creative activities not so much by love for others, but by a creative need, by a love for beauty or even by prosaic motives such as money, fame, popularity, etc. Notwithstanding the absence of agapic love in the activities of these great creators, their works have had powerful effects on generations of people in terms of gratuity, trust and civilization. Although they were not subjective benefactors, they became, objectively, educators of humanity, contributing to making the history of humanity more civil. In these cases the inadequacy varies from extreme situations in which there is no motivation for loving, to intermediate cases in which love is one among the various motivations, to situations in which agapic motivation is dominant and finds its expression in actions and objectives reached. In the case of Perlasca, we can observe an elevated level of inadequacy between his intentions, which are not consciously agapic, and his behaviors and agapic overabundance, which renders him particularly effective in saving human lives.

Sorokin's penta-dimensional system is useful in order to render the concept of *agape* operational, thereby allowing the possibility for empirical analysis of social facts. We will use the five dimensions as categorical variables and non-metric ones, as is prevalently done, maintaining that *agape* has particular difficulty being used as a quantitative variable (Montesperelli, 2011). This system would enable us to offer some coordinates of proximity of the greatness of *agape* and it would make its empirical manifestation identifiable and intelligible. This penta-dimensional system would also allow for both the comparison between different socio-cultural contexts and the definition of the various forms of *agape*, and to classify the types and the activities, the subjects who carry it out, the interweaving within typologies and the most frequent combinations of a given social group. Lastly, such an operationalization would allow us to establish and to study functional as well as causal relationships, and the meaning between the dimensional variables here considered.

Agape, in fact, expresses that very piece of social reality ignored by the sociological lexicon and which renders 'anomalous' social phenomenon. It is the reality of overabundance, its every antecedent, a kind of action that Simmel has already numbered among the primary motivations for social action, this last one being non reducible to the egoism-altruism continuum, in as much as the extremes of I and you are only the prerequisites of the social, not able to be simplified to the elements composing it. For this very reason *agape* is always a social concept. There can be no *agape* without society, that is, without there being the other, and therefore, without a social relationship and interaction. Even when *agape* is neither of these two things, but is social action, it is characterized as such for the meaning attributed to it by a subject. The symbolic order being a collective elaboration, it always precedes the use that the individual makes of it and for such argumentation then, *agape* in never even an atomistic concept.

# 1.6 Six agapic propositions

After having defined *agape* and pinpointed the typical traits of its actions (its renouncement of equivalence, present moment, processes, language, absence of anticipation, silence of desire), and having traced its dimensions, we proceed to delineate some propositions of the concept which we propose with the aim of helping the empirical phase.

*1st Proposition: Agape as the primary motivation for action*

A first feature is suggested by the timeless Simmel: action oriented by love as the primary motivation is foreign to the conflict between selfish action and altruistic action. This is an intuition he proposes in the *Fragmente über die Liebe* ([1921] 2001), published post-mortem and which belongs to the last phase of Simmelian thought, characterized at once by an existential and social reflection.

Simmel shows how egoism and altruism are the extremes on the human motivation continuum, because *agape* is not reducible to either end of the two extremes. It is possible that social action out of love be independent from that alternative. It abolishes every distance between the 'I' and the 'you.' In Simmel's words, the specific peculiarity of love concerns the fact that it "doesn't eliminate the being for oneself of the 'I,' nor that of the 'you,' but rather makes it a prerequisite based on which the elimination of distance is accomplished" (p. 161). In this interpenetration we find a more general feature of Simmel's analysis regarding an order of questions which deal with sociology's statute, which a century ago was expressed by the question: 'How is society possible?' Its answer was that society is a unity at once between being produced by society, being members of it and the intimacy of the subjects. From the combination of these three elements empirical society is formed. To be for oneself and to be for sociality form an altogether, the person in his/her totality, who cannot do without these three belongings for his/her very existence.

Rather, there is a different interplay, according to the form that relations brought about by them assume (the meeting between a client and a clerk in a bank, two friends or two people who love each other). The three dimensions, *being for one self, being a member*, and the *beyond* of every person, define the field of action of each one, in which one experiences the dimension of being creator and being created by society, of being father and son, but also something more (society transformed). All of this is empirical society which therefore can be subject to observation (Simmel, 1989, pp. 32-36).

*2nd Proposition: Agape as interpenetration by the subjects creates social institutions*

What happens when sociality becomes the product of intimacy and its members act by putting *agape* as a foundation to their actions?

Niklas Luhmann, even though in a context of love such as eros, elaborates the concept, which particularly useful for our research objectives, of system of interpretation to view sociality created by an action that is the product of two subjects who freely choose to live one for the other. In this case, love is a relationship of mutual penetration in the life of Alter and Ego, which is at the base of living and experiencing. Each one, in the moment in which he turns towards the world of the other, is himself changed, or rather, every subject is transformed and becomes part of his object. Moreover, the 'object' does not remain still, but assumes the action in itself, accepting to be transformed in turn. Such mechanisms, although separated analytically, happen contemporaneously, empirically speaking: "self-reproduction and hetero-reproduction remain, according to systematic contexts, separate, and are however done uno actu" (Luhmann, 1987, p. 234). Love, then, is a primary and irreducible action because with its action it determines its own object and creates it as a particular object which did not exist before its loving. But at the same time, the one who loves is different from the one he was previously, before he started to act out of love. In this way, we understand unity of agapic action, because love, in the moment in which it is lived towards each neighbor, recreates the subject and the object at the same time: 'As far as I'm concerned, there exists no other sentiment in which the absoluteness of its object, in whom the *terminus a quo* and the *terminus ad quem*, though in their insurmountable opposition, join themselves so unconditionally in a current which is not fed at any point by an intermediate event (Simmel, 2001, pp. 169-170).

Therefore, people's agapic action produces a reality *sui generis*, a unity between subjects which in reciprocal agapic action flows into a generative and proper social, which Boltanski would call state of peace, but which in the dynamic here delineated is different, in so far as the subjects are not foreign to one another, do not suspend self-reflection, do not omit the use of faculties in order to live the other, but are its prerequisites: social action becomes relationship. Nevertheless, to express this created social reality, it seems heuristically more meaningful to go to Archer's concept of *emergent property*, in other words, to the fact that each dimension is able to develop autonomously its own characteristics and abilities:

> "Emergent properties can be entities of distinct nature, such as capital, rent, inflation, or the educational field, for example, which take part within the social structure, since they depend essentially on material order components. Other emergent properties are Buddhism, neo-liberalism... which participate in the cultural sphere" (p. 178).

Agapic action, by putting itself at the crossroad between intimacy, being members and products of society, constitutes the structure and social agency and hence, a proper social reality.

*3rd Proposition: Agape and its tragic aspect*

But love, so as to assure the *interpenetration* of lives within a context of personal freedom, which produces emergent properties, contains within itself a *tragic* aspect. It is Simmel again to indicate this suggestion. Agapic action is founded on a contradiction between the sentiment of loving the other, aimed at building an interpenetrating sociality, and embracing the other till one 'loses' oneself in him. But in this very moment, *agape*, in generating the other from oneself (in loving him) is making an act of creation that is estranged or actually opposed to the reality of the one who generated it (the reality of non-love). Furthermore, the tragedy of love is in its very law, which is accomplished in generating the other from oneself, that which is foreign and actually opposed, especially in relation to the world in which, often, it does not find space, but from which it drew strength for its birth and its conservation. The martyrs of love have often been accused by the world of apostasy, unfaithfulness and blasphemy, because their love is universal and not particular. The particular world to which they belonged constituted 'orthodox committees' which in the course of history have condemned witnesses of *agape* in the name of the principles those martyrs advocated. Agape is destined to become a 'subversive enemy' and to be persecuted by those who love their very particular world (Sorokin, 2005): Socrates (469 B.C.-399 B.C.) was condemned to death by tribal Athenian patriots; Jesus was crucified by Hebrew tribal patriots; the Muslim prophet Al Hallaj (850-922) was burned by Muslim patriots; Gandhi (1868-1948) was shot by Hindu orthodox for his non-violent activities; Isaac Rabin (1922-1995) was a martyr of peace for having extended his hand to Palestinians.

*4th Proposition: Agape transcends the life and action of those who produce it*

Other than these quite frequent cases of heroism, *agape* produces a reality that transcends the life that it brings about It creates, that is, a reality that is different from the previous one in which both Alter and Ego were immersed, before acting out of love for one another. The destiny of agapic action is the breaking of bridges that were built for the journey, and to recognize in this breaking its most intimate necessity. Peter Berger in his *Homo Ridens* (another type adding itself) describes some sociological traits of transcendence which we can use for our concept of love. Agape transcends the reality of ordinary existence because it postulates, although temporarily, and alongside other action modalities, a different reality in which principles and rules of common life are suspended. This is the aspect of sociological transcendence, certainly in a minor tone in view of philosophical and theological questions on this argument. Yet, some manifestations of agapic love makes one think that this 'other' reality has redemptive virtues that have nothing temporary about them, or which remand to that 'other world' that is always possible.

In *Homo Ridens* one talks about a 'freeing laugh.' To explain the transcendence of the comical, Berger refers to Alfred Schutz, showing how it irrupts in the conscience of daily reality, which we share and which therefore imposes itself as real. The daily state is a heavy, irresistible reality, one that imposes itself. Humor is subtle, at times shared, at others not. It is a 'limited sphere of meaning,' or like an island in the ocean of daily experience. There is a whole series of experiences similar to this: the world of dreams, of a theoretical reflection, of an aesthetic experience, of physical pain, of an ecstatic experience, etc. All these islands of meaning have common characteristics: they have distinct categories of space and time, they have distinct orders of reality, experiences of their boundary of entry and exit, etc. (Berger, 1999, pp. 293-308). Agape brings us to transcend this daily reality because it is not routine, it is not a typified one, but contrarily, the subject is ever ready to go towards new shores, new experiences for whomsoever passes by him and can ask of him.

*5th Proposition: Agape as action in freedom breaks the rules and juridical formalization*

In this sense, *agape* annuls law. Kierkegaard (1813-1855), in fact, in his reflection on acts of love, shows how 'necessity' substitutes 'completion' (Kierkegaard, 1983, pp.90-94). In fact, by its very nature, law needs continuous specifications, interpretations and application mediations, because it is a recall to ever new needs, whereas love's action is foundational, not generative of disputes, but generating authority through its acts. Releasing itself from any formalization, from intentionality of judgment towards the other, it frees him from any possibility of dispute. Agape has a rule that is internalized and its validity is founded by the intentionality of loving and does not prescribe anything on others. For this reason it does not seek to overthrow a scene, nor does it expect recognition by the public or the people, thereby freeing its subjects from the anguish of having to return what has been received. For this reason, *agape* is rooted in minimal gestures, in seemingly most insignificant actions: for example, by going to get the milk in the place of a younger sister who has little desire to go to the store, while a storm rages about outside on a cold winter night.

*6th Proposition: Agape roots itself in daily living, its privileged place*

At the same time *agape* roots itself in the *daily life* of every person, and this is its place of predilection. Daily life, in Gouldner's sense (1997), contains within an idea that society is the product of small collective realities of human existence, producing social change starting from its subjects, refuting the idea that transformation is exclusively a leader's prerogative. Heroic culture, in fact, being founded on the proof of its value, denies the recognition and the dignity of others: 'daily life is a counter-concept, representing a criticism of a certain lifestyle, the heroic one in particular, aimed at realizing an existence centered on a series of trials. Daily life affirmed itself as real in counter-opposition to the heroic one in view of its crisis' (pp.39-40).

Instead, *agape*, rooted in daily living, frees from the anguish of having to prove one's heroism and hence, from the desperation of waiting for the other to do likewise. Anguish and desperation, the life-ill of our times, are foreign to *agape*, because the decision to love is not founded on waiting for reciprocity, or on the expectation of a reward from the other, or even a judgment by the other on such behavior. Acting out of love, notes Kierkegaard, doesn't depend on the other's love, since its interiority does not expect recompense (Kierkegaard, op. cit., p. 120).

## 1.7 Conclusion

In this chapter we have put the bases for a new category in traditional sociology which is *agape*. We started from a brief review of the recent presence of the concept of love in sociological literature to successively presenting the pioneering work of Boltanski, and before him, that of Sorokin regarding the topic of *agape*. But we went beyond, proceeding to a formalization of this concept, and to the definition of five dimensions capable of making it useful for empirical analysis, and we elaborated six propositions which deal with its relationship with the social context of reference. Along this pathway we inserted research in the scientific tradition of social sciences which looks to empirical reality as a foundational moment of sociological knowledge, inclining every reference to a meta-physical hypothesis of the concept.

# Chapter 2

# What Agape is not

In this chapter, we will trace out the conceptual difference of *agape* from other concepts close to it. Such work is necessary in keeping with the cautiousness of the science, that is, when not necessary, the introduction of new constructs must be reduced. New definitions of love begin to appear, that is, the Platonic eros and the Aristotelian philia, to then pause on decisively more sociological concepts, such as that of gift according to the tradition of Mauss and that of solidarity, all in order to put into relief that none are easily assimilated by or in some way express a sense that renders the concept of *agape* superfluous.

## 2.1 Eros

According to Hellenistic mythology, the god Eros was generated in very ancient times, a time, that is, just following the one in which only Caos and Gea existed. Indeed, Parmenides considered Eros as the first among the gods. Eros was begotten by his father Poros (Expediency), and mother Penia (Privation, lack of); from Poros he inherited a desire for the good and the beautiful and also the ability to procure them for himself (Poros was the son of Methis, goddess of perspicacity); from his mother he received, instead, the condition of lacking these goods. According to Plato, this tension was the most fitting metaphor of philosophy, tending between aspiration for knowledge and the awareness of a condition of privation, between being conscious of one's lack of knowledge and the inability to fulfill it (*Simposio*, 203 B-206 A (T.6)).

Among his multiple functions, is the task of mediating between mortal and immortal reality, of reducing in such a way the hiatus between the gods and humans; in order to do this he functions as an 'interpreter and messenger for the gods on humans' behalf and for humans on behalf of the gods (*Simposio*, 202e). Therefore, Eros has a hermeneutical function: like Hermes, he also translates the will of the gods, rendering it more intelligible to men, allowing them to transcend themselves and turn their attention towards the divine. The original concept of 'hermeneutics' lies very much in this interpretation/translation of the divine into the human.

But hermeneutics is not only the transposing of a language into another – more or less difficult to do and always interpretative – (Ricoeur, 1999/2001, pp. 51-74). Both Eros and Hermes are messengers who go beyond the confines of two worlds, to put Olympus in touch with humanity, or better – in Platonic terms – the world of ideas and perceivable reality. In other words, hermeneutics is also going beyond the delimitation already given. In Hermes this becomes more evident through his transgressive behavior, breaking with taboos and violating constituted rules (Burkert, 1977/2010, pp. 309 ss). For Eros, instead, going beyond what is 'normal' takes on a profile of untamable passion: there is an inexhaustible tension itching to fill the privations of existence; and such tension is wrought even in the search of knowledge, in love and in wisdom (*Simposio*, *passim*).

The Platonic eros concerns the definition of a criterion of equivalence and of general accountability that is at the base of this type of social tie. Plato expresses his idea of love-eros in *Fedro* and in *Simposio*, in which he shows that within the desire to have something one feels deprived of lies the foundation of its own manifestation. Eros, attracted in the first place by something beautiful and, hence, beautiful bodies, shows himself dependent on the beings he turns to, and therefore he can descend to a lower level: 'to the urge of pleasure' (*Platone*, 1993, p. 130). But he can also turn to the heights and lift himself up towards the celestial eros, renouncing immediate possession, to contemplate perfection in the world of ideas. Thus, sense having such a root, it brings this conception of love to build a dualism of sense-ideas, founding in turn a tension that is irreducible in a particular-general relationship. Consequently, to be fulfilled, love-eros must break ties with the particular and rise up to the general; only along this pathway can one adhere to a common superior principle. In this way, Plato substitutes love towards concrete subjects with a general principle of equality between individuals. The theory of Eros is tied to the political theory of justice which should inspire city leaders (*Platone*, 1974). This erotic mania, belonging to Plato's philosophy, maintains the violence of the first-born of eros, at the foundation of many theogonies, as non-generated, without principle, and therefore ungovernable by reason and by logos.

Eros has to do with market economy. In fact, Georg Simmel, in his *Philosophie des Geldes* of 1900, points out that money is modern economy's code founded on finance. Money becomes the mediator that has real power and an infinite symbolic meaning. From this moment onward, everything – people, sentiments, aesthetics, morals, space and time – take on a measurable value. In following Simmel's reasoning, we find ourselves realizing that money is indifferent to differences and makes us equal. By reusing the categories of love, we can say that money is erotic, meaning that it allows the appeasing of needs and desires through continuous annexing of properties of things with which we recompose a unity, which in its premise flows from the solitude of significant relationships (Simmel, 1984).

The official tradition of economic science which, from the point of view of expressed sociality is still profoundly Smithsonian, bases itself on the assumptions of mutual indifference: the intention of A's action is completely independent from B: A satisfies B's preferences only as a means to achieve his/her own individual objectives: there is no need to hypothesize any form of belonging to a communitarian reality, to an 'us.'

From this point of view, if we take the classical distinction of love and of human relationships in eros, philia, and *agape*, economic science of Smithsonian inheritance is all defined by the eros concept. That which pushes the entrepreneur towards intrepreneurship is, particularly in the beginning, the force of eros, of desire, the will to fill a lack of honor, wealth and power (Bruni, 2009).

The Medieval period has been the great incubator of the market economy. Medieval fides and philia had finished carrying out their function of mediators in commercial and financial exchanges in Europe with the Protestant Reformation (by Luther but also Calvin and other reformers). In Medieval times and civil humanism, in fact, the market had been a network of personal relationships that were not anonymous ones, amongst people who knew one another. Trust was placed on people made of flesh and bones, upon their identities and histories. This mercantile ethic made Florence, Venice, Marseilles and Bruges great.

From the mid-fifteen hundreds, after the civil and religious wars among Christians, Europe wanted to find a new base for its exchanges, for a new Europe with new social bonds, and fides was no longer needed: it was enough to think about one's own interests and the good of the other as well as the common good would emerge indirectly from the interaction of these. The market found thus its universal vocation (typical of Illuminism), and while no longer

limited by philia and fides, could now open itself to anyone, founding a new egalitarian and liberal humanism, where every individual
interacts potentially with all, without truly encountering anyone, if
not oneself.

Thus in the sixteen hundreds merchants and states gave life to a
new market economy (at least for exchanges between cities and between States) that was increasingly anonymous and financial, where
it was no longer the people and their identities to circulate within
Europe (as well as in the New World), but, instead, abstractions such
as credit titles, paper money and transactions. Starting from there,
the market begins to be impersonal and becomes a form of relationship carrying out its function of mediator among unknowns.
Capitalism is born in this new season for Europe, where exchanged
goods lose any contact with the identity of the people who created
them.

The invention of the monetary market has permitted a huge ex-
pansion of exchanges and the inclusion of millions to billions of
people today, thanks to its disempowerment of human relationships
and of any personal element that bespoke of difference, true diversity (religious, ethnic and national...). In order to do an exchange
with another, one need not know the other in his deep being: the
pricing system imposes itself as a 'third' actor, sterilizing the meaningful relationship founded on recognition. This brings about the
ambivalence of the modern and more contemporary market: the
disempowering and leveling of human diversity makes possible an
exchange with any 'other.' One no longer needs fides or philia: desires and reciprocal needs are enough, a kind of relationing, even
this universal one, that can be similarly associated with eros. At the
same time, this universalism is not a network of encounters among
the diverse, but rather, relationships that are mutually indifferent
amongst subjects, as they are rendered homogenous in order to allow the exchange, without difference or one that annuls the diversi-
ties. The eros of the market allows one to annex and possess through
money. The extraordinary innovative and inclusive power of the
market and its great ability to produce solitude and anomy are both
the result of the invention of modern economy: the erotic exchange
that is expressed in our society of debt and consumerism, which
consequently brings alienation, solitude and anomy, as well as the
insolvency and credit crunch of this time.

The agapic relationship, that is, the bond between different people, has been relegated to the private sphere, an ever tightening one,

or to situations of resistance and to humiliating and degrading conditions.

## 2.2 Philia

In Aristotle we find a second declination of the love bond, called philia, expressed in the *Etica Nicomachea*, in which friendship manifests itself precisely in reciprocity of action (*Aristotele*, 1987). In Aristotle, friendship has a political meaning and is not relegated to private relationships among people. It precedes justice, therefore, because it is founded on the recognition of reciprocal merits, which are interactively communicated (ibid., p. 395): for this reason, the co-presence of friends is important, who cannot remain distant in space and time (ibid., p. 387). The typical element of love-philia is reciprocal benevolence, which presupposes a common measuring system, a principle of equivalence, which permits the reciprocity of exchanges, of appreciation and evaluation of merits, according to a shared rule of equality (ibid., p. 400).

Therefore, the Aristotelian conception of philia presupposes a principle of accountability which sustains the friendly interaction oscillating between the evaluation of merits and the reciprocity of behaviors, a circle tying one to the other, hence, in philein there is intimacy but not the sweeping passion that fogs up or obscures reason and logos, such as in eros. Boltanski shows us that love-*agape* is a notion belonging to Christian theological tradition, but in being a sociologist he is interested in looking "at the way in which the regular relationship between men can be regulated" (Boltanski, op. cit., p. 54). In Christian theology the concept of *agape* designates, first of all, God's relationship with men, but it applies also to relationships that humans have among themselves, which finds a tie with the idea of unmotivated love, given without keeping track of merits or demerits (Nygren, 1990, pp. 93 e 96; Von Balthasar H., 1981).

The notion of love-*agape* is different from love-eros and from love-philia, because on the one hand, it does not imply the dimension of desiring something that is missing typical of eros, while on the other, it is indifferent to merit and to the object's value in which it finds a resemblance in some way, this last being an element that characterizes philia. Along this line, the pure idea of humanity is unknown to *agape*, in the sense of altruism professed by laicized religions of positivism as posited by Comte, because, as Jean Brun

refers to in the French introduction to Kierkegaard, the second theoretical source for Boltanski (Kierkegaard, 1983), *agape* is not born
"from an imperative deriving from the universality of a law... [since]
it looks towards the neighbour" (Brun, 1980). The concept of neighbor for *agape* is not associated to relationships of familiar proximity,
of group or nationality, but to each object whose eye it meets, and
for this reason, is detached from any identifying particularity.

A great thinker of Western culture has reasoned on the paradox of
philia. In fact, Nietzsche points out the quintessence of friendship
in a relationship of co-belonging, in which the drama consists of the
fact that the distinction, the twosome, is absolutely insurmountable. Distance is safe in absolute co-belonging. This relationship
is clear in a passage from *Gaia Scienza* entitled *Star Friendship* (Nietzsche, 1985, p. 279). The friends are two ships, each keeping its
own route, but constantly far and near. They protect each other,
save each other and love each other. Thus, proximity and distance
without ever confusing the other. They are the opposite of equal,
of pares. The two ships have different routes, yet they never lose
each other because friendships guarantees them distance, but a distance that is co-belonging. Therefore, we can fully comprehend the
step of love towards one's neighbor in Zarathustra (Nietzsche, op.
cit., pp. 70-1), in which this is a presentiment of the *über* that indicates the need to go beyond man, meaning that Nietzschian image
in which is expressed a criticism to all the metaphysical-humanistic
traditions. The figure representing fully the trait of 'beyond-man'
is that of the friend, in this case uprooting all the tradition of the
history of philosophy. In the *über* Nietzsche thinks of the absolute
negation of any possessive relationship, giving a place to the different and the distinct. In the 'beyond-man' one thinks of the radical
gift in its absolute gratuitousness, and this is the negation of hu-
manistic tradition and, therefore, also of the tradition that thinks of
friendship as a relationship of *inter pares*, as a relationship of equality. Here, the friend is the one who perceives his relationship with
the other as that which constitutes their difference. This idea is of
the utmost importance because it introduces us to the deep understanding of the meaning of 'beyond-man'. Nietzsche, however, in
recognizing the insufficiency of the concept of philia as equality, of
the Western philosophical tradition, redefines its contents. On the
heuristic plane, it is most useful to transfer these contents to the
concept of *agape*. In this way, we can better understand the criticism given on the social level, on the one hand, to Plato's eros, be-

cause eros is the instinct to recompose the one, to be the one to annul any difference that thinks itself originary, while on the other hand, also the philia, as it presupposes a relationship *inter pares*, among equals, is likewise a danger to the emancipation of the subjects. Instead, *agape*, by founding its bonds on overabundance, roots its origin in the otherness of each. This way, one recognizes the distance from the other and in this distance one is together: a *communitas* is created with the emancipation of each one as its premise. Agape creates the communitarian space, meaning those intersubjective bonds of co-belonging that do not confuse, identify, or make equal. Subjects of *agape* are with the other, which is their commonality: one, two, and the common, that which is neither of the one nor of the other. Only in agapic action can we found an idea of *communitas*, but of the ancient star. Since any other idea of love, would throw us once more either into the erotic dimension of desire-annexation, or in the philiac dimension of camaraderie, of that which is equal, annulling the oppositions and the differences, that, instead, *agape* recognizes and in which it roots its essence.

## 2.3 Gift

To justify introducing *agape*, in our view, we should see whether the social we intend to express could be interpreted by a concept close to *agape*: that of gift. According to us, gift is not able to bring to the fore, describe, or explain that observable reality which instead could be expressed by *agape*, but not because there is a more or a less, but simply because they are interpretative tools, each able to enlighten different aspects of reality.

First of all, we must agree on the concept in question: when we talk about gift we refer, at least in this faculty, to the theoretical tradition that has been consolidated in social sciences beginning with the essay by Mauss (1965, and or. 1923-24). Mauss considered gift as a sort of exchange typical of archaic society. Such an affirmation is not an interpretation of texts by Mauss, but is explicated right in his *Essay on Gift*, whose subtitle declares: *Form and Reason for Exchange in Arcaic Societies*. Ulterior support for this definition of gift, intended as a form of exchange, is in another paper by Mauss: *Exchanged Gifts and the Obligation to Give in Return*, in which is shown that gift: "...presupposes 1) the obligation to give; 2) the obligation to receive; 3) the obligation to give back" (*op. cit.*, p.172). The study by Mauss utilizes the concept of exchanged gifts to interpret economic transactions of *Potlach*, that is, of the system of exchanged gifts between pre-literate populations of the Tobriand Islands, which imply not only that the doner gives and the donee receives, but that the social obligation (norm) exists of maintaining the duties of each:

> "...the total transaction not only implies the obliga-
> tion of giving back gifts received; but it also supposes
> two others equally important: the obligation of giving,
> on the one hand, and an obligation of receiving, on the
> other" (*op. cit.*, p.161).

In this instance, the giving connects the giver, the gift, and the donee in a relationship of reciprocity, which, defined or undefined in time, expects restitution according to its logic.

The presence of gratuitousness in this type of relationship doesn't change the model of action.

It is necessary to keep to this logic of exchange if we wish to understand the specificity of the concept of gift. Starting, then, from its original meaning we will show successively how the contradictions of gift, not only stimulate, but give space to the need for defining a concept in *agape* useful to social sciences. For criticism on the concept of gift, we look at work done by Jacques Derrida, *Given Time : Counterfeit Money* (1992). In this essay, the French philosopher shows the contradictions of gift to the point of drawing away giving from any form of gift, meant as exchange, till making it vanish as a phenomenon in its definition of gratuitousness. In the first place, Derrida shows that: "While there is gift, there should be no reciprocity" (ibid., p.14), because giving makes the gift part of an economical regime: one of offering, of paying a debt, of giving back a loan, all according to a calculation mentality, for interest, usefulness, etc. Instead, where there is giving, every exchange should be suspended (ibid., p.14).

The author also shows a second argument for the contradiction of gift:

> "While there is giving, the donee should not give back,
> amortize, reimburse, get rid of debt, enter into a con-
> tract with, or never have incurred a debt" (ibid., pp. 15-
> 16).

In this case, Derrida is not talking about an ungrateful person, but refers to the unawareness on the part of the giver of having to give, who doesn't see and doesn't know that a gift has been received. In this sense, Derrida wants to express also the necessity of not making the gift dependent, as a social phenomenon, on the recipient's conscience, affirming in this way that the phenomenon of gift exists also where the recipient is not aware of it. In the third place, Derrida asserts:

> "... this unawareness of the gift must be radical not only on the part of the donee, but first of all on the part of the donor."

That is, Derrida shows how the conscience of gift annuls the gift itself:

> "...the gratifying image of the goodness or generosity of the giving being who, knowing himself as such, recognizes himself circularly, speculatively, in a sort of self-recognition, of self-approval, and of narcissistic gratitude" (ibid., pp. 25-26 and pp. 147-148).

In fact, Mauss, in his definition of gift, showed this definition of narcissistic power of gift, of a return of conscience to itself which establishes an immanent economic exchange: "giving equals showing one's superiority, being worth more, being higher up, *magister*; to accept without giving back in excess, equals subordinating oneself, becoming a client or servant, making oneself small, falling lower (*minister*)" (Mauss, *op. cit.*, p. 281). Therefore, for there to be gift, the ego of the giver should be annulled, as giving becomes possible only by losing oneself. In the fourth place, in order for there to be authentic giving, according to Derrida the gift itself should disappear:

> "...the subject and the object are the gift's stoppers" (ibid., p. 26).

With this affirmation, Derrida intends to show that the moment in which the gift appears as such, meaning, it is objectified, it would make the giving disappear. This doesn't imply that if the gift did not objectify it would lose its empiricism, but that manifesting itself to the conscience of the recipient and of the giver would make it come into the logic of an economic exchange and would extradite it from the range of donation. This is why he previously affirmed:

> "It could be gift, meant as gift, only by not being present
> as gift... If it presents itself, it is no longer presented"
> (ibid., pp. 16 and 17).

With the four arguments of contradiction of gift by Mauss, Derrida shows two contradictions: the first affirms that, either the gift presents itself as such and thereby disappears because it gets raised to a system of economic exchange (just as Mauss intended it), or the gift is no longer presented, it disappears, but in this case it exits as a phenomenon, intended as an empirical dimension of giving. Therefore, if it appears, the gift is presented as an exchange not belonging to the market; if it doesn't appear, it disappears. In this dimension, giving is lost to social science as a useful concept. In our view, the contradictions shown by Derrida – and so as not to fall in the same – open a breach to the need of introducing the concept of *agape* in social sciences (we can define that gift, in fact, as *agape*, because it is overabundant, it disappears, and in disappearing, since it cares not to be returned and/or for the merits of each one, it is then affirmed). Such a necessity doesn't respond to metaphysical, theological or philosophical reasons, according to which as sociologists we would not have the tools to support these reasons. Rather, the concept of *agape* in social sciences would permit us to interpret all those social phenomenon of absence of calculation, of unconditional action, of non-usefulness, of absence of reciprocity (in the moral conscience of both giver and receiver) and of restitution, of overabundance, without motive or interest, starting from itself, which gift, as understood by Mauss onwards, could not interpret. Therefore, we wish to propose the idea that the possibility of gift is indeed the exchange without mediation of money, and its impossibility or disappearance, discussed by Derrida, is the possibility given by *agape*. In fact, bottomless giving, as intended by Thomas Aquinas:

> "... is verily a donation without return ... that which
> is given without intention of restitution" (cit. in Marion,
> 2001, p.102)

since it is not present in the tradition of ethnic-sociological studies (and if it were it would have those same contradictions expressed by Derrida), it is necessary then to use a new concept, such as *agape*, in order to express the action, the relationship and the social interaction that, as such, is without return, restitution, uncaring of merit or demerit, bottomless, and allow gift to interpret all those realities of economic exchange and reciprocity not mediated by money, or at least not mediated just by money.

## 2.4 Conclusion

In questioning concept of *agape*, we asked ourselves if it could not be assimilated to close logical constructs and therefore we investigated what *agape* is not, looking at other forms of love such as eros and philia, but we have seen that *agape* does not overlap the concept of gift. Agape is not eros because it is not characterized by the motive of desire. Nor does it resemble philia because this is made typical by the reciprocity of the action. Literature on gift is very abundant and complicated to wean, as it has two traditions: the socio-anthropological and the theological. The two concepts have different meanings and traditions. We have dialogued with that reflection held up by the circuit of giving-receiving-restitution, starting with Mauss, we have found the contradictions contained in Derrida's criticism, and we have defined the heuristic space of *agape*.

Chapter 3

# Love in the sociological tradition

In this chapter we will be looking at some classic figures of sociological thought to see if there are agapic traits in their proposed social analysis. We will look at Simmel, Weber and Sorokin because in these authors we feel there is a discussion on the merit of the concept with which we are dealing. Simmel, in particular, and more so Sorokin, concern themselves specifically with the topic of love in its agapic meaning as well. Instead, in Weber, the reconstruction is more complex, to be retraced in many parts of his complex work, but not less evident for it, and above all fundamental to discovering the importance of his reflection on Western modernity.

## 3.1 Georg Simmel

Simmel (1858-1918) is considered one of the 'teachers' of sociology. Though he founded no school of thought, his intellectual heredity was very fertile, as he himself was aware of:

> "I know that I will die without spiritual heirs (and that's fine). My heredity is like coin money, which can be divided up among many heirs, each investing his part according to his nature, without being interested in its origin" (Simmel 1970, p.11).

Simmel was born in 1858 in the center of Berlin from Jewish parents, and later converted to Catholicism. The last of seven siblings, he lost his father early and his education was entrusted to a rich family friend. He studied history at the *Gimnasium* and then philosophy at the University of Berlin and in 1881 pursued his doctorate in philosophy. His students found him to be a very fascinating teacher and his lessons were overflowing with young people who, after a few years would influence the European cultural panorama. Among them we recall Mannheim, Luckacs, Bloch, Small, Park, Kracauer and Banfi. In 1914 he obtained a university teaching role at the mature age of 56, in the suburban University of Strasburg. However, due to the breakout of World War I all academic activities were suspended (Dahme, Rammstedt, 1984a, 1984b).

At that very time Simmel published his papers on the American Journal of Sociology of Albion Small, on the "*Annee Sociologique*" by Durkheim, and became a member of Renè Warms International Institute of Sociology. His own students were instrumental in bringing him fame. Simmel became one of the main theoretical references of the School of Chicago (Levine et al., 1976). His popularity in the United States declined along with the loss of centrality of the School of Chicago when, starting from the mid thirties, American sociology became functionalist due to the publication by Parsons of The Social Structure of Social Action (Parsons, 1937).

Only at the end of the sixties were studies resumed, and the knowledge and utilization of Simmel's interpretative categories saw a new day due to new sociological theories such as symbolic inter-actionism (Blumer, 1969) and ethno-methodology (Garfinkle, 1967), which picked up once again on Simmel's interpretative perspectives and the fundamental notion of social interaction. The rebuilding of his cultural heredity is a complex operation, because of his eclectic studies. He was interested in philosophy, art, history, science, and religion, besides sociology. From amongst his copious scientific production, the purely sociological works to be considered are: *The Social Differentiation* of 1890, *The Problems of Philosophy of History* of 1892, Philosophy of Money, of 1900, *Sociology* of 1908, and *Forms and Games of Society* of 1917.

In his unfinished paper *Fragmente über die Liebe*, posthumoulsy published in 1921, the topic of love is fully within the themes dearest to Simmel; to occupy oneself with it meant to go to the center of those questions that involved his entire intellectual journey. In fact, in this paper as well, the question is always the same: how society is possible and how it is built on the basis of interaction between people.

The other point that keeps cropping up is relative to the question investing the conciliation and the synergy that comes about between the psychological-individual dimension and the sociological one. Having put up these sign posts, to speak of love is equal to speaking of social action starting from human sentiments, or better, from the essential element, putting said sentiments as a factor, so to say, at the forefront of the formation of society. Love is qualified as the main viatic in the formation of relationships, society's prince of sentiments. As a consequence, love, as the sentiment retained to be the most intimate, permits the passage from the individual plane to beyond-the-individual, the collective one.

To face the topic of the building of sociality based on an approach adopting as a starting point the sentiment of love, offers the further advantage of keeping track of how the subject relations himself to the external environment, amplifying moreover the range of action of the loving sentiment to the inclinations, predispositions of spirit, also those leanings of the subject himself in regards to inanimate things, for this reason, Simmel retains love to be "an immanent function, and I myself would say a formal one, of psychic life" (Simmel, 2001, p. 167). Regarding this, the sociologist from Berlin excludes from love's characteristics all that, to him, does not contribute to designate such a sentiment. In the first place, the counter-opposition between egoism and altruism, as elements able to establish the contours of love, does not convince him; secondly, it explicitly moves away from the rational notion of Schopenhauer as a modality for treating such a topic; lastly, it excludes an anchoring of love to instincts, sustaining that even if there were a tie between the two terms, the question is very different, as you will see, in reality.

Relative to the narrow definition of love, what we can take away is that it is characterized by the fact that it allows for an establishing of a relationship. However, it is a specific relationship, because it is made possible due to overcoming the distance between two subjects, distinct from one another, brought face to face. It is almost too banal to observe how the idea of the overcoming of two such different entities, finding themselves in opposition, gives place, if not to a superior synthesis, then to a different condition, one of major breadth compared to the initial situation (Bianco, 2011).

Therefore, in a Simmelian vision, according to which love puts two different subjects face to face, thus bringing about unity from diversity, the amorous sentiment represents the base for collective life and, being configured as a modality of externalization of the *Wechselwirkung*, is presented as a sociological problem. In Simmel's words, the specific peculiarity of love concerns the fact that it:

> "...does not eliminate the being in himself, neither the I nor the you, but rather, it makes it a prerequisite on the basis of which the elimination of distance is accomplished" (ibidem., p. 161).

In this interpretation we find a piece of analysis by Simmel that is more general, regarding an order of questions dealing with the statute of sociology, which a century ago was expressed by the question: "How is society possible?" His answer was that society is at once a unity between being *produced* by society, being *members of it*, and the *intimacy* of the subjects. Empirical society takes its form from the combination of these three elements. Being for oneself and being social, together with the intimacy of individuals (Archer calls it interior conversation) form an altogether, the person in his/her totality, who cannot do without, for his/her very existence, these three kinds of belongings. Rather, they have different impacts, according to the types of relationships s/he establishes (the meeting between a client and a clerk in a bank, two friends, or two people who love each other). The three dimensions, being for one self, being a member of, and the beyond of every person, define the field of action for each person, in which one experiences the dimension of being creator and being created by society, of being father and son, but also something more (society is transformed). All of this is empirical society, which therefore can be subject to observation (Simmel, 1989, pp.32-36).

True acting out of love, its authentic manifestation, sees the 'I' and the 'you' brought face to face; the 'I' is leaning against the 'you' in he attempt to abolish the existing distance and to adhere to the 'you,' thereby forming unity between the subjects. The irreducible distinction between two people who meet is presupposed by love, which tends toward going beyond such a barrier. It is sentiment that allows for such a 'miracle' (Simmel, 2001, 161); therefore, this does not come about in virtue of the ability of the interested party, nor by his/her rational representations. On the basis of the relationship between the 'I' and the 'you,' and how it is modulated, social relationships are built and so are judgments on what is right and what is wrong. Such a relationship then acts as a compass in our relating with the world, or better, as Simmel sustains, it constitutes its "absolute matter" (Simmel 2001: 159). The social interaction that has at its base affectionate action has always been interpreted as oscillating between two poles, that of altruism and of egoism, bringing into the latter also being moved by instincts. Simmel retains, on the one hand, that egoistic behavior is oriented by 'I,' and on the other, that the one driven by instinct responds to laws of nature and consequently does not have that kind of orientation. According to Simmel, altruistic action on its part should not be equated to acting out of love, because, in truth, this latter can be considered as much altruistic as egoistic. Referring to altruistic motives par excellence – those of a religious type, or of human and social solidarity, which generally urges one to act for someone's or humanity's good – Simmel sustains that one is on a more general plane in respect to a direct involvement by two actors; that one be in some way active and moved by superior ideals, be they abstract from context and contingencies.

As to the dynamic interesting the actors in the relationship, Simmel retains that love is a process that transforms the object of the sentiment, as well as the one feeling such a sentiment. In fact, the person being loved is determined by the love, or better yet, s/he acquires sense and meaning in being the object of love. Before the circumstance of being loved, the person loved did not exist. Love makes its subject appear under a different light, in a certain sense it shapes it, building it as an original representation.

Love then is a primary and irreducible action because with its action it determines its own object and creates it as a particular one, which did not exist before being loved. Yet, at the same time, the one doing the loving is different from the one s/he was previously, that is, before starting to act out of love. In this sense, we understand the unity of agapic action, because love, in the moment in which it is lived towards each neighbor, recreates both the subject and the object at the same time:

> "As far as I'm concerned, there exists no other senti-
> ment in which the absoluteness of its object, in whom
> the *terminus a quo* and the *terminus ad quem*, though
> in their insurmountable opposition, join themselves so
> unconditionally in a current which is not fed at any point
> by an intermediate request event" (Simmel, 2001, pp.169-
> 170).

Love then does not depend on the quality of the loved one, quality that would justify said love revealing the exclusive character of love, which is a subjective event and doesn't put mediation between the subject and the object of love, notwithstanding the opposition between the two terms. Even the subject who feels the sentiment of love is different in the moment in which he loves, because the wholeness of the person is taken by the sentiment, though not showing any external evidence of it. Love is possible because such sentiment is internal to the subject who loves, 'in a latent state' or in hibernation, and does not manifest itself as an element induced or solicited from something external. Rather, it seems to be a vital force pushing the subject towards others, towards constructive interaction with his like, favoring his attachment to the world. This inclination would be a resource that is activated, precedent to a full unveiling of a predisposition already inherent in the subject and translated into behavior. In the final analysis, love is nothing but the elaboration of our relationship with the world and in this relating, which involves our psychic life, the subject enjoys the maximum freedom. Simmel also deals with the other aspect of love: the tension between individuality and generality. Having met apropos the insufficiency of philosophy Simmel turns to literature, taking a cue from two couples in the works of Goethe: that of *Faust* and Margaret in Faust and that of Edward and Ottilia in *The Elective Affinities*. It deals with two distinct types of love: in *Faust* love is of a general type, meaning that the protagonist's love is not turned towards his woman in her specificity as a person, but rather to a female being in general. In the second case, that of Edward and Ottilia, love is directed to a specific individuality (Simmel, 2001, p. 179; Vozza, 2001, p. 106).

Edward and Ottilia represent individual love, or love turned exclusively towards that specific object of love and to no other individuals; it is about a sentiment that in some ways remands to absolute love. This latter is concentrated on the single case and is aimed only at it. In a certain sense, love can call itself absolute when it has no other aim than the object loved, considering it in its uniqueness. However, the fact of retaining a loved person to be irreplaceable channels the sentiment onto tracks that could lead towards a growing individualization.

The topic of individualization, in its modern version is taken up and developed also in the *excursus* contained in the *Fragment*, where the analysis by Simmel goes from Plato to Christianity (Vozza, 2001, pp. 106-107). First of all one must observe that for Simmel the Platonic concept turns out to be in opposition with the modern one, which is characterized by dynamism. Simmel notices that love, according to Plato, is not a spontaneous move of the soul, it does not represent a way for it to express its own vitality, but is raised by the contemplation of beauty because it recalls a primordial beauty (Simmel 2001: 184 and sgg.), and therefore it seems to be a rational consequence of the encounter with beauty. For Plato the amorous sentiment has fixed and atemporal characteristics, resolving itself in an eternal dimension. In its turn, beauty, in the Platonic perspective, allows the conjoining of the earthly element with the ideal one so that perceptible experience is able to bond with the ideal world.

Philosophy is the instrument by which one can understand all of this. If for Plato beauty is something to be admired, the concept of beauty for modern humans is instead much more immanent, it being tied to a person, and is thereby inseparable and intrinsic to a specific subject and contextualized in reference to the emotions and sensations it arouses.

The other aspect Simmel indicates as a censure between Plato and modern people is represented by the fact that the first does not conceive reciprocity and therefore excludes relationship; to the contrary, "for modern love the authentic goal is to be corresponded to". For modern people, love is a relationship of 'I' with the world. Contributing to this is also the fact that the representation of the world is the fruit of an activity of the conscience of modern humans, who attribute meaning to surrounding reality. In the field of modern culture, it is the dynamic internal to the subject – "a free act of the soul" – which feeds reactions, elaborations, and therefore also "visions of the world." Regarding this, Simmel speaks curiously about "productivity of the modern soul," much more reactive in comparison with the classical one and able to "exercise a continuous creative activity." Consequently, in modernity love is a possibility for relationship in so far as "mediation between men" (understood to mean people) while "Greek eros is desire for possession ..." (Simmel, 2001, pp. 184-186).

To explain better how individuality is reconciled, or the peculiarity of a love relationship and the sense and spirit of love according to modern culture, Simmel adds that relationships between single individuals have a specific meaning only for actors who give rise to said relationship; at the same time though, the meaning of their bond, even if generated by the peculiarity of that experience, goes beyond such confines and assumes general contours. Simmel intends to sustain that sentimental relationships undergo a shift from the category of the particular to that of the general. In the most intense phase of passion, this is perceived as something absolutely without equal (Simmel, 1989, p. 582). However, when the idea of the loved one and of one's own sentiment is re-dimensioned, when the sense of uniqueness and of exclusivity of the relationship takes on common characteristics as those of any other amorous relationship, when the same relationship takes on a more objective dimension, then a process of maturation and of objectivation of the amorous passion is begun. The passage from the inter-individual plane – or better, from the specific concrete case – to the beyond-individual one that allows for the creation of society is an obviously dear topic to Simmel. Notwithstanding the differences of the conception of love and of beauty between the ancient and the modern, Simmel retains that something of the Platonic idea of love has survived into modernity. In fact, notwithstanding how much the modern conception of love is turned towards the single person and the individual plane, our culture still cultivates the conviction, inherited by Plato, that love is a sentiment capable of transcending simple daily contingencies of life.

## 3.2 Max Weber

Max Weber (1864-1920) is one of two classic sociologists who have had the most influence on the discipline's development. His scientific research has opened up new fields of study in politics, law, economy, music, religion and cities, just to indicate the main ones. Weber has lived a great existential tension between the dimension of the scholar of social reality and that of political involvement, by which he intended to change the course of events. He observed with disillusionment the direction of social changes of modern industrial society, noticing how the world was becoming more constrictive due to bureaucracy and rationality. A great part of Weber's monumental work can be considered a dialogue with Karl Marx's ghost, while the other part would be with Friedrich Nietzsche. Weber did not hold the view that social change should always directly follow economic changes. Other factors, such as religious ideas, could assume an independent role as well. His methodological writings, in which he shows the need for a sociologist to be always be nonjudgmental in his scientific work, assumed great importance; that is to say, that his own personal convictions and inclinations should never insinuate themselves into research and into his conclusions.

Therefore, for a renowned thinker's monumental study on modernity, characterized by de-personalization and rationalization of social relationships, it can seem strange or even contradictory to find within the work of Max Weber an ample and enlightened examination of love. Weber places particular attention on 'fraternal love,' which is a type of love that is religious in its origins and has its roots in the concern of the universality of human suffering. The amplest discussion of this love, and the ethical position emerging from it, is found in *Intermediate Reflections* (Weber [1915] 1948b), titled: *Re-*

*ligious Rejections of the World and Their Directions*, a text that has been amply discussed in interpretative literature and which has been considered the central text in the understanding of Weber (for example, Tenbruck 1980; Turner 1991; Bellah 1999). Surprisingly, even if love is manifestly the topmost topic in this crucial work, the ethic deriving from religious love has been almost kept quiet by scholars of Weber's works.

Our discussion on love in Weber's works does not propose to affirm some new unifying principle for his works, but limits itself to recalling attention to a dimension of love that we retain has been neglected in interpretative literature, even with represented exceptions by Ballah (op. cit.) and, above all, by Symonds and Pudsey (2006).

In particular, these last two scholars are very important because they have identified in Weber's sociology the concept of fraternity (brotherhood) as effect of love in universal religions. We will use this study with the goal of adapting it to our aim to understand.

While the concept of love is very visible and discussed in *Intermediate Reflections* and is very present in the *Introduction to the Economic Ethics of the World Religions*, entitled *Psychology of the World Religions* in the edited edition by Gerth and Mills (Weber [1915] 1948a), as well as in sections on religion and power in *Economy and Society* (Weber [1921] 1978), it is also subtly and variously used in his empirical studies on the world's religions. In these works, a complex typology of love emerges and allows Weber to trace the paradoxical destinies of a series of empirical forms of the bond of love in the world, within different processes of cultural rationalization. In particular, four main types of love can be identified in Weber's studies: Puritan; Mystical; Christian-Medieval; and Charismatic-communitarian. Weber contrasts these different types of 'love' in a more general, ideal-type form. To understand this typology and the different types of identifying love, it is necessary to go back to the two works containing his most explicit discussion on love, *Intermediate Reflections*, and in a lesser degree, *Introduction to the Economic Ethics of the World Religions*.

Weber never explains the precise nature of this model of love which brings to universal fraternity, however, on the basis of his observations in *Intermediate Reflections* and through an examination of his religious sociology, we retain that it is possible to ascertain five important dimensions of this historical ideal-type. In the first place, it has a universal reach and is applicable to all human beings, who all share in the common condition of suffering. Secondly, it maintains a personal or ethical recognition of the suffering of others, underlining the direct, face-to-face dimension of the caring for someone. Thirdly, it is kept in a state of tension with the orders of the world and, as a consequence, turns away worldly orders because they are imperfect, thus becoming a general love without an object, or acosmic (cfr. Bellah, 1999, for an extended discussion of the meaning of 'acosmism'). Based on such orientation, only the suffering of other human beings is retained to be important in this world. Finally, he is intransigent in dealing with the world and he refuses to accept any other position as valid or of useful value: in this sense his view acts as an ethic of end goals and convictions.

The main historical form of love is that of charismatic communitarianism (of which we will be speaking later on), which is closer to the ideal-type, even if it does not enter completely in the canons regarding the dimension of universality. The characteristics of Weber's ideal-type of love are five: universality, personal recognition and consequent care for, the refusal of compromises with other ethical types, together with a referral to the first religious and communist communities, as explicitly expressed in this passage by Weber:

"The principle constituting communal relations among the salvation prophecies was the suffering common to all believers. And this was the case whether the suffering actually existed or was a constant threat, whether it was external or internal. The more the imperatives issuing from the ethic of reciprocity among neighbors were raised, the more rational the conception of salvation became, and the more it was sublimated into an ethic of absolute ends. Externally, such commands rose to a communism of loving brethren; internally they rose to the attitude of *caritas*, love for the sufferer per se, for one's neighbor, for man, and finally for the enemy ... In religions of salvation, the profound and quiet bliss of all heroes of acosmic benevolence has always been fused with a charitable realization of the natural imperfections of all human doings, including one's own. The psychological tone as well as the rational, ethical interpretation of this inner attitude can vary widely. But its ethical demand has always lain in the direction of a universalist brotherhood, which goes beyond all barriers of societal associations, often including one's own faith". ([1915] 1948b, p. 330).

Weber shows that for the religions of redemption, the presence in this world of unjustified suffering of the innocent is proof that existence is substantially an irrational place. Attempts to resolve and understand the problem of suffering have been the drawing power of all great religions, in which the fundamental element is the development of the ethic of fraternal love ([1915] 1948a, pp. 272, 275, [1921] 1978, p. 518). Weber shows that such an ethic emerges when "the magical ties and exclusiveness of the sibs have been shattered" ([1915] 1948b, p. 329; see also [1921] 1978, p. 361) and are replaced by a faith fraternity. The citation reported above indicates that the origins of this religious love are to be traced back to the ethic of the closeness of communities of hunters, village inhabitants and fishermen ([1915] 1948b, p. 361, [1921] 1978, p. 361), which underlined the obligation of giving help and alms to people in difficulty within the community. Weber comes up with an illustration of this social phenomenon in his study on Judaic tradition (Weber [1917-1919] 1952, pp. 64, 67, 342-43). For those brought together by suffering, love is transformed into an intransigent ethic of absolute end, putting itself in direct conflict with the order of the world and its sphere of values of those who pursue such ideals, especially when these acts are rationalized according to worldly logic. In fact, this is the central theme of *Intermediate Reflections*: "The tension between brotherly religion and the world has been most obvious in the economic sphere" ([1915] 1948b, p. 331), "The consistent brotherly ethic of salvation religions has come into an equally sharp tension with the political orders of the world" ([1915] 1948b, p. 333); "Above all there is tension between the ethic of brotherliness and the spheres of aesthetic and erotic life" ([1915] 1948b, p. 341); and there is a last internal tension between religion and intellectual life ([1915] 1948b, p. 352).

All those forms of love which bring about fraternal bonds are in tension with the erotic sphere, the esthetic and intellectual ones, but some are able to overcome this tension with the political and economic order of the world. This last point is of crucial importance in differentiating the types of love. Within the origins of an ethic of fraternal love, numerous historical forces have created a variety of empirical forms of love. Weber's work runs through these historical trajectories and, as has been said, seems to concentrate on four main empirical forms of love – the types one finds, as mentioned, are those of Puritanism, Mysticism, of Organic Medieval social ethics and of the first Charismatic Communities.

Throughout all of Weber's work, we find that these types, in their historical manifestation, lose one or more of the characterizing aspects of the ideal-type – universalism, personalism, acosmism, the tension with the world and a refusal to compromise with it.

Let us then look at the four ideal-types of love: 1) Puritan, 2) Mystical, 3) Organic, 4) Charismatic.

### Puritan love

Puritan love contrasts with the ideal-type form on four of the five dimensions. Weber identifies two main tendencies in particular which brings it in direct contrast with the ideal-type of love. To begin with, the ideal of universalism is in clear contrast with the idea of 'fraternity' found in sects of virtuous religious, like those found in the beginning of Protestantism (especially in America), such as *The Protestant Sects and the Spirit of Capitalism* (Weber [1906, 1920] 1948c), which shows that a much more limited form of love developed within Protestantism when the idea of universal suffering was abandoned and the confines of group membership was recognized by the proof of ones' own state of grace. This protestant form of love could be defined as 'sect love', which is based on an obligation of care given only to 'brothers' in the faith (Weber [1906, 1920] 1948c, pp. 308, 318-19) and is against the universalism of the 'church' ([1915] 1948a, p. 288, [1921]).

Secondly, the logic of Puritan love abandons the personal aspect, because it refuses the ethic of recognition of common suffering. For Weber the meaning of "personal" is about relationships between people in which an ethical dimension is possible. Every purely personal relationship of man (person) for man (person), of any type, even one of complete servitude, can be subjected to ethical requirements, and be ethically regulated. This is true since the structure of these relationships depend on individual wills of the participants, leaving space to such relationships for the manifestation of love itself ([1921] 1978, p. 585).

The process of rationalization of the economy in Capitalism and of politics expressed by bureaucratic power is clearly the biggest source of immoral impersonality. In fact, in the political field "the political man (person) acts just like the economic man, in a matter-of-fact manner, 'without regard to the person,' *sine ira et studio*, without hate, and therefore without love. By virtue of depersonalization, the bureaucratic state, in important points is less accessible to substantive moralization than were the patriarchal orders of the past..." ([1915] 1948b, p. 334; see also [1921] 1978, pp. 600-01, p. 975). Weber's analysis of the Puritan vocation examines how this religion has encouraged its followers to operate "without regards for the person," for the effect of giving love and care in the name of the recognized grace of God ([1921] 1978, p. 1200; Weber [1915] 1951, pp. 236, 241, 245).

For Weber, the characteristic of impersonality is a logical consequence of the Puritan conceptualization of predestination: the plan of God cannot be known and not even put in doubt; the one in need doesn't need to be helped because s/he contests the creation of the order of God's world; moreover s/he who is in need deserves his suffering.

There is no longer any regard for the person and his pain, rather, even charity is aimed at promoting work and the market. Fraternity presents itself without love. Furthermore, the elect consider "the sin of one's neighbour" not in terms of "sympathetic understanding," but through "hatred and contempt for him as an enemy of God bearing the signs of eternal damnation" (Weber [1904, 1920] 1985:122). Fraternal love now includes elements of hate when the ethical preoccupation for the suffering of every person is replaced by the search for grace that is manifested in professional success. At least in radical Protestant types of people, these two dimensions – the impersonality of Capitalism and the refusal by the elect to maintain personal ethical relationships of help and care for others – can co-exist without conflict and perhaps also in harmony, according to the celebrated thesis that Weber sustains with regards to the birth of Capitalism. The acosmism of the refusal of the world of the first religions of salvation is thereby inverted. Work as a vocation becomes the center of the economy itself, and the absolute moral standard.

For the Calvinist:

> "Brotherly love, since it may only be practiced for the Glory of God and not in service of the flesh, is expressed in the first place in the fulfillment of the daily tasks given by the '*lex naturae*,' and in the process this fulfillment assumes a peculiarly objective and impersonal character, that of service in the interest of rational organization of our social environment. For the wonderfully purposeful organization and arrangement of this cosmos is, according to both the revelation of the Bible and to natural intuition, evidently designed by God to serve the utility of the human race. This makes labor in the service of impersonal social usefulness appear to promote the glory of God and hence to be willed by

him" (Weber [1904, 1920] 1985, pp. 108-09).

This forsaking of universality and of personal recognition led to a coherence of "charity without love" ([1915] 1948 b, p. 359) which is summarized in the following passage:

> "As a religion of virtuosos, Puritanism renounced the universalism of love, and rationally routinized all work in this world into serving God's will and testing one's state of grace" ([1915] 1948b, p. 332).

With impersonal relationships tending towards exclusion, Puritan love eliminates tensions with the economic and political world, as opposed to what other religions were able to do. Puritan professional logic allows for participation in the economic sphere, permitting this particular form of love and fraternity. Puritanism interprets the will of God as: "commandments should be imposed upon the creatural world by the means of this world, namely violence" ([1915] 1948b, p. 336), and this means that it is in a state of "consummated threat of violence, war" ([1915] 1948b, p. 335), which can be reconciled with the Puritan ethic.

In this manner, Puritan love is impersonal, exclusive, intra-worldly, and without internal tension in dealing with the economic and political world. However, at the same time it maintains an ethic without compromises in full pursuit of these aspects of its theology. Briefly, the internal logic of Puritan love tends towards a position of extreme contrast with the ideal-type of love.

### Mystical love

A principal form of empirical love examined by Weber is the mystical love. Mystical forms of love maintain an acosmic dimension, that is, of a universalism without compromises but tending towards the impersonal as does the Puritan form. Such character of impersonality allows this type of love to avoid tension with both the economic and the political world. Once again, intellectualized coherence is the reason for such impersonality and it allows the avoidance of tension with worldly orders. In its more coherent form, acosmism brings a complete refusal of worldly logic, among which, consequently, a refusal of human beings as deserving subjects for recognition. From an ideal-type point of view, this seems to be the basis of the problem regarding mystical love. Mystical love denies the world and its subjects because whoever happens to cross one's

path becomes the subject of devotion and love. Therefore, it is indifferent to merits and demerits ([1915] 1948b, pp. 333, 336). "The
postulate of (mystical) fraternal love" is, then, extended to a "completely non-selective generosity" ([1921] 1978, p. 589). Such a love
reaches a height of impersonality in so much as the real person and
his/her suffering are not a source of worry:

> "the mystic's 'benevolence' ... does not at all enquire
> into the man to whom and for whom it sacrifices. Ulti-
> mately, mysticism is not interested in his person. Once
> and for all, the benevolent mystic gives his shirt when
> he is asked for his coat, by anybody who accidentally
> happens to come his way and merely because he hap-
> pens to come his way. Mysticism is a unique escape
> from this world in the form of an objectless devotion
> to anybody, not for the man's sake but purely for devo-
> tion's sake, or in Baudelaire's words, for the sake of the
> 'soul's sacred prostitution'" ([1915] 1948b, p. 333; see
> also [1921] 1978, p. 589 , [1915] 1948a, p. 289).

This type's motivation is not personal love or the answer to the great
problem of suffering, but the mystic's own salvation. Mystical love,
according to Weber, "involves a search for individual salvation in
the emotional state of love for love's sake. All people are treated
equally as merely a means toward this end." For this reason, from
the point of view of an ethic of love that maintains a certain sense of
subjectivity, the other's importance and his suffering will be judged
as essentially egoistical. These points in the analysis are reinforced
by Weber's examination of fraternal mystical love found in Buddhism.
According to Weber, Buddhism has a "cool temperance" (Weber [1916-
1917] 1958, p. 208, [1916-1917] 1996, p. 332), which "guarantees the
internal detachment from all 'thirst' for the world and men" (Weber
[1916-1917] 1958, p. 208; see also [1921] 1978, p.628). Here, and only
here, lies real salvation. An altruistic ethic of universal compassion
is only a step on the road towards enlightenment:

> "the specific form of Buddhist 'altruism,' universal
> compassion, is merely one stage which sensitivity passes
> when seeing through the nonsense of the struggle for
> existence of all individuals in the wheel of life, a sign of
> progressive intellectual enlightenment, not, however, an
> expression of active brotherliness. In the rules for con-
> templation, compassion is expressly defined as being

replaced, in the final state of mind, by the stoic equa-
nimity of the knowing man" (Weber [1916-1917] 1958,
p. 213).

Buddhist love, in its detachment, reaches extreme points of impersonality. In fact, it is characterized by the same impersonality and
concreteness comparable to Jainism, and in other respects, to Puritanism. The personal, *certitudo salutis*, not the well being of ones'
neighbor, is the problem (Weber [1916-1917] 1958, p. 209). For Weber, Buddhism therefore represents the most important coherent
example of mystical love, characterized by universal impersonality.

An ulterior important distinction should be drafted into the type of
acosmic love. In *Intermediate Reflections*, Weber identifies in Bud-
dha, Jesus and St. Francis, three religious expressions founded on
love ([1915] 1948b, p. 357). All three could be taken as examples of
acosmic love [1921] 1978, pp. 540, 552 for St. Francis). Buddhism,
instead, is also interpreted along an extreme logic of mystical eva-
sion of love ([1921] 1978, pp. 627-28, [1915] 1948b, pp. 339-40). Weber distinguishes, then, Buddhist mysticism from some Christian
manifestations of acosmism.

This is confirmed in the study on Buddhism in which he affirms
that: "The concept of neighborly love, at least in the sense of the
great Christian virtuosi of brotherliness is unknown" (Weber [1916-
1917] 1958, p. 208). Both can be defined as religions of fraternal
acosmic love, but they are qualitatively different in practice and in
the type of faith. The citations reported here suggest that Christian
acosmic love is relatively "hot," more active and expressing more
closeness to the subjects than other forms of oriental love, which are
from this point of view more similar to the coldness of Puritanism.
Weber does not specify beyond this contrast, but some pointers expressing this difference can be deduced.

All Acosmic mystics, be they Eastern and Western, have an evaluation criterion of their neighbor that is characterized by impersonality. However, the virtuous Christian – despite the adoption of an
acosmic stance and indifference towards the world ([1921] 1978, pp.
630-33) – will never go all the way to reach the highest point of pure
mystic indifference towards their neighbor. So, even though both
Jesus and Buddhism "evoke the most radical demands for the ethic
of brotherly love" ([1921] 1978, p. 593), and although Jesus adopts
a "mystically conditioned acosmism of love" ([1921] 1978, p. 633),
there are significant differences in terms of religious rationalization.

Jesus is considered to be a magician by Weber ([1921] 1978, pp. 630-
31), in the sense that an important difference applies to love that
maintains attention to detail, in fact the "charisma of the pure 'mystic' [serves] only himself [while the] charisma of the genuine magician serves others" ([1915], 1948b, p. 290). Furthermore, the acosmic vision of Jesus is mixed in a manner that is inconsistent with
elements of the Jewish religion ([1921], 1978, p. 633). This relative
inconsistency is combined with the underscoring done by Weber
with respect to the active nature of Western Acosmism, which pri-
marily expresses itself in working in the world and, therefore, in the
presence of ascetics who are God's instruments, rather than "vases
of the divine" ([ 1915], 1948b, p. 285).

Being active in a world that is simultaneously denied, rather than
following the path of contemplative retreat, allows the form of Christian love to have a more direct involvement with suffering. For these
reasons, one can infer that Christian acosmic love can be contrasted
with Eastern variants. In this sense, the Christian who lives the virtue
of brotherly love may be closer to the ideal-type of pure mysticism,
in as much as his/her love is active, relatively "warm" and expresses
closeness to the suffering person.

Mystical love distinguishes itself from the ideal-type form since its
retirement from the world includes the elimination of tension with
the economy and politics, while maintaining, in accordance with
the ideal-type form, an uncompromising stance in terms of its own
theological consistency. Since all that is worldly is denied, there is
no other interest in it – neither into any aspect of economic life nor
in political life – for one's only goal is personal salvation (as above,
[1915], 1948b, p. 333; [1921], 1978, p. 589).

To summarize, the most significant mystical forms of love are universal and reject the world; they are uncompromising, impersonal
and without tension with the economic and political world.

### Social-Organic Love

The third great historical expression of love that Weber discusses
is a form of organic social ethics, which is universal, personal and
in tension with the world even though it looks for ongoing compromises. Unlike the acosmic direction of mystical love, this organic
ethics – the one seeking brotherly love – has a cosmic orientation.

> "Organic social ethics, where religiously sub-structured,
> stands on the soil of 'brotherliness,' but, in contrast to
> mystic and acosmic love, is dominated by a cosmic, ra-

tional demand for brotherliness. Its point of departure
is the experience of the inequality of religious charisma.
The very fact that the holy should be accessible only
to some and not to all is unbearable to organic social
ethics" ([1915], 1948b, p. 338).

Even if he makes a brief reference to the professional Lutheran life
as a vocation, Weber's main discussion is about the hierarchical vision of things, based on medieval "organic social ethics," which is
related to Thomas Aquinas ([1915], 1948b, pp. 338-39; [1921], 1978,
pp. 597-601). Within this conservative perspective of things, the social world is imagined as ordained by God and founded on the basis
that, on one hand, presupposes social inequality among human beings and, on the other hand, equality with respect to suffering. This
reality is based on a relatively rational order, despite its wickedness,
in as much as there are at least traces of the divine plan in the world.
Herein lies the cosmic dimension, which includes the position to
accept the world and the commitment to improve it ([1915], 1948b,
pp.338-39). For Weber, perhaps in this doctrine lies the most important sociological reason of the church as a factor of "democratic"
impetus ([1915], 1948a, p. 288), which is obviously contrary to the
exclusiveness of the virtuous sect (Weber [1906 and 1920], 1948c,
pp. 308, 318-19, [1916-1917], 1958, pp. 201-02). Such a medieval
Catholic doctrine is in this sense universal.

Upon this organic ethics was based, for a certain period of time,
the rationalization of the Western economic and political world.
During the Medieval phase of Western social development, the economic and political spheres had not yet reached the state of impersonality which they attained within modernity. Thus Weber highlights that they were able to maintain a personal dimension of love
and brotherhood.

"The medieval and Lutheran traditionalistic ethics
of vocation actually rested on a general presupposition,
one that is increasingly rare, which both share with the
Confucian ethic: that power relationships in both the
economic and political spheres have a purely personal
character .... These relationships of domination had a
character to which one may apply ethical requirements
in the same way that one applies them to every other
purely personal relationship" ([1921], 1978, p. 600).

Lutheran vocationalism, according to Weber, is to be linked to the social form of Medieval organic social ethics, which can be recognized by its openness to a personal relationship. In fact, from Luther up to a certain point, work was specifically justified through love, because "the division of labour forces every individual to work for others" (Weber [1904 1920] 1985:81). Weber describes this as being "highly naive" (1985, p. 81), and suggests that, for Luther, vocation would have been the element that was needed to justify work as the only way of life acceptable in the eyes of God. This perspective, from Luther's standpoint, is very conservative and traditionalist. In fact, the individual must always remain in the place where God has put him, and must maintain his worldly activities within the limits imposed on him by his position in life. Although his economic traditionalism was originally the result of the indifferent love of Saint Paul, it later became the result of an ever more ardent faith in divine providence, which he found in an absolute obedience to God's will (Weber [1904 and 1920] 1985, p. 85). In other words, Luther had initially conceived professional work specifically in terms of love for one's neighbor (= neighbor), but later changed this position by accepting the organic traditionalist vision of the given and hierarchical order of social reality, which finds its roots in the form of vocational ethics of Medieval Catholicism.

In this latest Lutheran version of vocation, the ethics of love towards one's brother is no longer its own justification, but finds its ethical potential in doing one's job well. And here – within personal relationships of work life in itself – the ethics of love can be pursued. Thus, Weber suggests, before the advent of modernity, personal and ethical relationships were possible within professional life, as a vocation, even though such a social order was based on inequality (Weber [1921] 1978, pp. 1006, 1013, 1025-1026 , 1028-1031, 1070, 1083, 1105, [1915] 1948b: 331).

Weber explains how, on a personal level, a universal ethics of brotherhood did empirically exist. However, since personal and universal relationships in which brotherly organic love could be pursued – that is, they were part of professional life – this period of the Christian Church entered into "relativities and compromises" with mundane spheres ([1915] 1948b, p. 331). Such a cosmic orientation, integration and compromise with the economic sphere must be judged harshly "as an accommodation to the privileged strata of this world," from the viewpoint of "the radical ethic of religious mystical brotherliness" ([1915] 1948b, p. 338). The tension between this mani-

festation of brotherliness and the world is strong. In all these am-
bivalent points: cosmic / acosmic; exclusive / universal; personal /
impersonal, the tension with the world is at its zenith. Such a conflict is highlighted in the contrasts between organic brotherly love
by cosmic ethics and by exclusive Puritanism, on one hand, and on
the other hand, by the acosmic mysticism of love. As illustrated by
the following quote:

> "The organic pragmatism of salvation must the re-
> demptory aristocracy of inner-worldly asceticism (as seen
> in Protestantism), with its rational de-personalization
> of life orders, as the hardest form of lovelessness and
> lack of brotherliness. It must consider the redemptory
> pragmatism of mysticism as a sublimated and, in truth,
> unbrotherly indulgence of the mystic's own charisma.
> The mystic's unmethodical and planless acosmism of
> love is viewed as a mere selfish means in the search for
> the mystic's own salvation. Both inner-worldly asceti-
> cism and mysticism ultimately condemn the social world
> to absolute meaninglessness, or at least they hold that
> God's aims concerning the social world are utterly in-
> comprehensible. The rationalism of organic doctrines
> of society cannot stand up under this idea, for it seeks
> to comprehend the world as an at least relatively ratio-
> nal cosmos in spite of all its wickedness" ([1915] 1948,
> pp. 338-39).

To summarize, Weber seems to argue that organic social ethics of
medieval Christianity (and of Lutheranism)have maintained an
ethics of universal brotherhood only because a historical meeting
of social forms and ideals would enable actual existence, even if it is
strongly compromised and tense, of such an ethics of being part of
the vocation to the world. The trend towards the universal and impersonal, within this ethics, has caused the loss of concern for the
suffering of others, to a greater extent than the one caused by the
autonomous logic of economic and political spheres.

### Charismatic Love
A final form of empirical love mentioned by Weber is the charismatic love. Even though this is the kind of love that is closer to the
ideal-type, it is the least preferred by Weber, mainly because it bears
no real historical significance for the birth of modernity. It related

only marginally to the central topics of *Intermediate Reflections* and, therefore, should perhaps be seen as relatively less important with respect to the other forms that were discussed.

As written above, for Weber, all religious ethics began with some form of love:

> "caritas, brotherhood and ethically imbued personal relations between master and servant ... remain the foundation of every ecclesiastic ethic, from Buddhism to Islam and Judaism and Christianity"([1921] 1978, p. 1188).

According to Weber, at the basis of all these religions, there is a common original source, the ethic of vicinity, of brotherly love for our neighbor. In addition, in this movement from the ethic of love of neighbor to the brotherly love of the religions of salvation, we go through the rejection of the world of universal brotherhood, to reach an ethic of brotherhood in terms of a "charismatic communism" ( [1921] 1978, p. 1187 , see also [1921] 1978, pp. 581, 1119-1120). Weber defines this first community as a "communism of loving brethren" ([1915] 1948b, p. 330).

Although this trait could be traced back in many religions, Weber particularly speaks about the groups that came about in the Middle East during the pre and early Christian period. In the *Ancient Judaism* sections, Weber speaks of the Essenes, and suggests that, although these groups lived according to a personal ethic of brotherhood, they were imbued with acosmic love and experienced a necessary tension with respect to the world. Furthermore, they were not inclusive when it came to recognize who were the people 'committed' in the world, which meant a fleeting existence of this ethic.

The Essenes, starting from the second century BC, were strictly detached from the world and rejected every economic possession that would go beyond their basic needs.

> "Correspondingly they pushed the old social commandment of brotherliness to the length of an unworldly love communism of consumption" (Weber [1917-1919] 1952, p. 407).

The ethics of the Essenes can be linked to the practices of the early Christian communities, which were characterized by a strict pacifism, by love of enemies and by "the communism of acosmic love" (Weber [1917-1919] 1952, p. 410).

Unlike the ethics of Lutheran and medieval vocation, which entered into an ethically problematic relationship with the forces of economics and politics, these early religious communities distanced themselves from the impure impersonal structures of society and tried to live an ethic of brotherly love without making any compromises with the world. Thus, within the fragmentation of society, they did not succumb to the socio-economic compromises of cosmic love and organic ethics. Moreover, these social organizations offered another variant of mystic love, because it is still able to maintain a personal ethic and is, consequently, not so "selfish" with respect to personal salvation. However, they were inherently unstable, not only because of the difficulty of maintaining the economic and political reality at bay, but because:

> "once the eschatological expectations fade, charismatic communism in all forms declines and retreats into monastic circles" ([1921] 1978, p. 1187).

These communities took shape around an indifference to the economic life / politics, an indifference based on charismatic religious expectations. But such an existence will be overtaken by the eventual turning of the charisma into a routine ([1921] 1978: Pt 1, Ch.111, v, see also [1921] 1978, p. 1121). As Weber states:

> "It is only in the initial stages and so long as the charismatic leader acts in a way which is completely outside everyday social organization, that it is possible for his followers to live communistically in a community of faith and enthusiasm .. ." ([1921] 1978, p. 249).

Such a radical love expressed itself in a distance from the world (acosmic), and yet, even though the community was held together by a charismatic religious authority, such a community could not endure for a long the distance between the lived and the worldly realities. This element helps to explain the relatively minor historical importance of the charismatic community of love. For Weber, however, they are at the same time a stage for more significant forms of religious fraternity. When confronted with the ideal type, a certain aristocratic exclusiveness of confraternities is evident, especially along the dimension of purity / impurity, notwithstanding the fact that this particular seeking of fraternity had been relatively contaminated by social and economic reality, and identified "a love of enemies" (Weber [1917-1919] 1952, p. 411). These early mystic communities paid attention to the personal dimension; they were acosmic and in conflict with the world, but they lacked the dimension of universality, which is another hallmark feature of the ideal-typical form of love.

## Conclusion

In order to understand the concept of love according to Weber, we had to delve into a number of his writings on the sociology of religion. Although this ethical issue is not a dominant theme in one of the major works such as *Intermediate Reflections*, a coherent line of thought can be put together. The ideal type of love is described by Weber as a sort of scale to measure the four main types of brotherliness that are present in many of his works: Puritanism, which is not based on a concept of company in suffering; Mystic love, which faces the suffering of others, but in an impersonal way, as in Buddhism; Cosmic love (as described in organic medieval Christianity), which, unlike the first two, builds bridges with the structures of the world through personal relationship with all those who suffer and, finally, the love of Charismatic communities, which have all of the characteristics of the ideal type of love, except for one clear Universalist option. Only cosmic medieval love has historically attempted to turn the world (mainly in the economic and political fields) towards an ethic of brotherly love, while seeking compromises ([1915] 1948, pp. 336-37). No one, neither the mystical community, nor the puritan type, nor the charismatic one, attempted to transform the world along the lines of such an ethic, but in their search for a mediating element, they were subjugated by economic and political orders.

All four types of love distance themselves from Weber's ideal type in one measure or another, going from the minimal distance of charismatic love, to the maximal distance of puritan love.

As Weber pointed it out, the ethic of love within modernity has left its traces in the "vocation" to science and politics. This normative discussion, however, goes beyond the scope of this paragraph, which has only been trying to put together the empirical descriptions of the ethics of love. What is clear is that the general use of the concept of love, in all the works of Weber, has a greater importance than what has been assigned to it by Weber's scholars.

# 3.3 Pitirim A. Sorokin

Pitirim A. Sorokin (1889-1968) is an important figure of the sociology of the twentieth century (Allen P.J., 1963). He was born in Russia
on January 21, 1889 in Turya, a small town located about 1,000 kilo-
meters northeast of St. Petersburg. His mother died when he was
three years old. Ten years later he was withdrawn from his father's
guardianship because he was an alcoholic. He was entrusted to his
uncle, who was a farmer and a very pious person. Sorokin absorbed
the spirituality and ethics of the Orthodox tradition, while working
hard in the fields. He was admitted to study at a school for teachers run by the Orthodox Church. At Khrenovc, political tensions
and his own poverty led Sorokin to become the leader of student
members of the anti-Tsarist Socialist Revolutionary Party. In 1906
he was arrested and spent five months in prison. Later on, while
freed but expelled from school, he went to St. Petersburg, where
still in poverty he continued his revolutionary action. In 1910 he
enrolled at the University of St. Petersburg and in 1916 received his
doctorate. His life was a fascinating one, full of tragedies and moments of exaltation. As a young man in Russia, he was imprisoned
first by the Tsarists and then by Bolshevik revolutionaries. He im-
migrated to the United States in 1923 to teach at the University of
Minnesota. He then founded the Department of Sociology at Harvard University in 1931, in which he started the Harvard Research
Center for Creative Altruism and held the most important Chair of
Sociology in the world. Sorokin stayed at Harvard until 1959, teaching several generations of important sociologists, but was opposed
to the ideas of the Social Darwinists and to those of the Chicago
School. Not even the ideas of Parsons' Social System were ever con-
sidered by Sorokin, so strong was the extent of his concern with the
anti-intellectual and technocratic drift of contemporary sociology.
Sorokin served as the 55th President of the American Sociological
Society. He died in Boston in 1968.

His thinking is complex. Sorokin considers society as a
well-structured system from a socio-cultural principle that gives
meaning and sense to all of the aspects of social life. This system
bases itself on three pillars: personality, society and culture. Social
life is therefore the superimposition of three elements: a physical-
chemical (inorganic) one, a vital biological (organic) one, and a mental (super-organic) one. The foundation of the socio-cultural phenomenon is the significant human interaction which consists of: 1)

the agent, 2) a material element acting as means of communication, 3) an intangible item, which is sub-divided in three aspects: meanings, norms and values. Such a concept of society as a system has caused the Sorokinian theory to be viewed as an organicism, even it is an organicism with cultural bases, not natural or biological ones (1947).

Sorokin, however, is best known for his studies on social mobility and stratification. He, in fact, developed in this area some conceptual tools that allow the interpretation of stratification and mobility along the economic, political and professional dimensions. From this point of view, Sorokin identifies social horizontal or vertical mobility, be it ascending or descending. In addition, the Russian-American sociologist identified the conditions that make possible, within a given society, a more or less intense mobility and its consequences (1927).

The universe is a reality containing three sensory-material elements, i.e. logical, rational and intuitive ones. These factors affect all forms of life and thought on the social level. At the historical level there are different phases, which are characterized by the predominance of one or the other. They start with the ideational phase in which intuition or faith prevails. They are followed by the idealistic stage in which truth is founded on reason. And then, they reach the sensorial phase, which is characterized by truth perceived by the senses. Such a period, characterized by selfishness and decadence, is the premise to the return to forms of knowledge and life marked by rationality and faith (1937-1941).

During his life, Sorokin felt the need to respond to this return to higher forms of knowledge, with respect to the sensorial phase. For this reason, he founded the Harvard Research Center in Creative Altruism, which promoted sociological surveys on the effectiveness of love as a creative force in relationships and social institutions. To understand human reality Sorokin elaborates a comprehensive method which consists in studying society by using three methods: empirical-sensorial quantitative, logical-rational and intuitive. It is only through the comprehensive use of these three methods that one gains a thorough understanding of historical complexity. Among the many writings of Sorokin we cite the most important ones: *Social Mobility* (1927), *Cultural and Social Dynamics* (1937), *Society, Culture and Personality* (1947), *The Ways and Power of Love (1954/2005).*

In *The Ways and Power of Love*, Sorokin examined seven aspects of

love, following the principles of comprehensive knowledge. The religious aspect of love identifies it with a Superior Presence. The ethical aspect of love identifies it with the good in itself. The ontological aspect of love defines it as a "force or creative energy that unifies, integrates and harmonizes," which works in different worlds; the physical, the organic and the psychosocial one (ibidem., p. 45). The physical aspect of love manifests itself in all the physical forces that unite, integrate and keep the entire inorganic cosmos in infinite units,
starting from the unit of the smallest atom to end up with the entire physical universe as a single unified and orderly cosmos (ibidem., p. 49). The biological aspect of love is evident in procreation and parenting. The sixth aspect of love is the psychological one, and that is where Sorokin defines love:

> "In every real psychological experience of love the ego or the 'I' of the individual who loves tends to be one and identifies itself with the 'you' who is object of his love. The stronger the love, the deeper is the identification" (ibidem., p. 50).

Sorokin also emphasizes that love conquers fear, as shown by the life of Gandhi, whom he admired, considering him as a modern saint:

> "Love is not afraid of anything or anyone, as it clearly cuts off cleanly the very roots of fear"(ibidem., p. 53)

and is associated with the deepest happiness and peace of mind. The seventh aspect of love is the social one:

> "At the social level love there is a significant interaction, or relationship, between two or more persons in which the aspirations and goals of a person are shared and supported in their implementation by other people" (ibidem., p. 55).

This is the first formalization of the concept of love that expresses a typicality linked to altruism, rather than to a logic that bases itself on keeping track of what has been given and received. It also excludes the idea that love can be an action, i.e. an act that starts from an originating subject with no return, or even only an individual one. In *The Ways and Power of Love*, Sorokin analyzes the psychological and social aspects of love and, in particular, developed a

five-dimensional model of love as a heuristic tool for empirical research. These are: intensity, extension overabundance, duration,
purity and adequacy. Besides allowing to empirically use the concept of the love of each individual or group, this method allows one
to develop different ideal types, such as for example high intensity
and limited extension, high intensity and short duration, limited
purity and long duration. This type of analysis enables researchers
to grade the:

> "types of activities of love and those who perform
> them, and understand which types and combinations
> are more frequent in a given human universe" (p.64).

The great charismatic leaders demonstrate high levels of each of the
dimensions: Jesus, Al Hallaj and Gandhi are emblematic empirical
cases. In the fourth Part, Sorokin defines ideal typologies of selfless and loving people. He, furthermore, also examines the various
processing altruistic techniques which are present in the religious
traditions of the world.

The final part of the book, *Tragedy and Transcendence of Tribal
Altruism*, is contained in only one chapter, Chapter XXIII, entitled:
*From Tribal Selfishness to Universal Altruism*. This is the last chapter, in which Sorokin expounds a universal law: "If selfless love does
not extend to all humanity, if it is confined within a group – a given
family, tribe, nation, race, religion political party, union, caste, social class or any part of humanity – this in-group altruism tends to
generate a corresponding 'out-group' antagonism. The more intense and exclusive the solidarity among the 'in-group' members,
the more inevitable are clashes between that group and the rest of
humanity. Herein lies the tragedy of tribal altruism which is not
extended to all humanity and to every person. The group's exclusive love makes members of the group indifferent or even aggressive towards other groups and outsiders" (ibidem., p. 647). This is
a bitter but realistic consideration and awareness of reality. Sorokin
is aware that violence and hatred find their origin in a fraternity
and love that only recognize its own kind. The Russian sociologist
hoped that science could make an important contribution towards
inventing techniques for the altruistic ennobling of individuals, of
social institutions and culture. As per Sorokin: "Science can help
us to attain the highest good of sublime love, which would have an
unlimited range, a maximum intensity, purity, durability and adequacy" (ibidem., p. 681). On the other hand, Sorokin denounced

the tendency of scholars to focus their research on the model of illness: "While many modern sociologists and psychologists considered the phenomena of hate, crime, war and mental illnesses as legitimate objects of scientific studies, at the same time they illogically stigmatized as theological preaching, or speculation, any non-scientific analysis of the phenomena of love, friendship, heroic acts and creative genius. This obviously unscientific position of many of my colleagues is nothing but a manifestation of the prevailing concentration on negative phenomena, pathological and subhuman ones, typical of the disintegrating phase of our sensualist culture" (Sorokin, 1963).

In February of 1949, Sorokin founded the Harvard Research Center in Creative Altruism with the donation of $100,000 from Eli Lilly. His first goal was to collect as much data as possible. In 1950 he published an important book entitled 'Altruistic Love: A Study of American Good Neighbors and Christian Saints,' which highlights the fact that "for decades Western social science has focused, *urbi et orbi*, on an ever deeper study of crime and criminals, of illnesses and the sick, of perversion ... and paid very little attention to positive types of human beings, their positive progress, their heroic actions and their positive relationships" (p. 4).

Four years later the book entitled '*The Ways and Power of Love*' was published. One can define it as the most important work of Sorokin, albeit not the most quoted one. The first Part presents the different aspects of love and empirical dimensions, which we mentioned, but also the methods of production, accumulation and distribution of the energy of love. The second part deals with a review of the theories of the structure of personality, as they are unable to interpret the altruistic dimension of human beings. The third part examines how and why the moral growth of the great figures of sublime love took place, building up some sort of classification of the selfless, and the factors that have influenced creative growth. The fourth part is a study of the main techniques of moral ennoblement, of yoga and the altruistic education used by monastic and secular brotherhoods. The final part proposes ways to move from individual and group individualism to universal love, in order to unite the human family.

The academic community expressed many reservations regarding the work on creative love, raising the criticism that it was a subject for philosophers or theologians, but not for scientists. These were years during which reigned the idea that disciplinary specialization was to prevail on multi-disciplinary approaches. From this point of view, Sorokin is a forerunner of changes sweeping the world's more advanced universities (Johnston, 1996, p. ix).

## 3.4 Conclusion

In this chapter, we tried our hand at meeting the great classics of sociological thought on the subject of love, and of the aspects that get close to the concept of *agape* as we have defined it. To our surprise, we saw that there is a relevant tradition of writings about love as *agape* by Simmel, Weber and Sorokin. We have seen some differences. On one hand, Simmel and Sorokin wrote about love. Sorokin even explicitly wrote about *agape*, while Simmel dealt with it as a part of his essay on the fragment on love. Weber, however, dealt with overabundance of love in his writings on the sociology of religion, but also here and there in the '*Intermediate Considerations*' and in the '*Preliminary Observations*,' as well as in the '*Introduction to the Economic Ethics of Universal Religions*.' While being part of the literature produced by the German sociologist, this is a dimension of his extensive work which remained hidden and was never rendered explicit by his own leading scholars and followers.

# Chapter 4

# The agape: the micro and the macro.

In this chapter we shall see that *agape* helps us in the interpretation of important social processes, at both micro and macro levels. In the first case , we shall see how *agape* is important in the process of the subject's formation. While we go down this path, we shall show present some interesting arguments as proposed by the philosopher Marion, the psychoanalyst Winnicott, and the social theorist Honneth.

In the second paragraph, however, using the genealogical research on modernity by Szakolczai, we shall draw on the concept of grace as *agape*, to highlight how this element is present at the roots of three major cultural traditions: the Greek, Jewish and Christian ones.

## 4.1 The subject, identity and inter-subjectivity.

Agape identifies a fundamental empirical process in the development of personal identity, especially in the early stages of life, but as we shall see, it is also a precondition for public participation. On the philosophical level, an important contribution was offered along this line by Jean Luc Marion, of which we shall use some epistemic elements for our interpretive journey (2001). Marion, having subverted the common concept of gift free from any lien of merchant reciprocity, which is a typical sequence of giving-receiving-returning, as we have outlined in Chapter 1, examines *agape* through a rigorous use of the phenomenological method, which starting from Edmund Husserl (1859-1938) and all the way to Alfred Schütz (1899-1959) was absorbed by the sociological tradition, outlining a new concept of donation, which at the conclusion of its reasoning identifies it as love, being the only process able to identify subjectivity, to allow for inter-subjectivity and to define individuality. In rebuilding his logical path, therefore, we shall use the concept of love in itself.

Marion starts by defining what a phenomenon is, identifying it as something that *manifests* itself and needs not be justified: "We dare to propose that the definition of the phenomenon as being what it manifests itself only to the extent that it *gives* itself, ensuring alone such a justification" (ibid., p. 393).

The phenomenology of love closes for the first time, in a radical manner, with the "subject"; neither destroying it, nor eliminating it, but turning it around, upside down. From a thinking and active "I," it finds itself as such as the "loved." According to Marion, only as much as they are *loved* can individuals proceed to the characterization of the "subject," which includes the gift of love, as a "figure of subjectivity granted through donation," i.e. the overabundance of love. "At the center there is no 'subject,' but a 'given one' (loved one); him whose function is to receive what is given without measure and, at the same time, receive itself from what it receives." It is, therefore, a person who receives in overabundance in the early stages of socialization, especially the primary one, and along this process constitutes his/her identity as a subject.

Therefore, the definition of the "loved one" enables a person to find a solution to the question of the access of the "I" to others, or to the problem of inter-subjectivity. The constituent subject of objects inevitably ended up closed within itself in a solipsistic manner, unable to meet others as others. The loved one, instead, who defines himself as the one who receives, and who receives himself from what has been given to him with no need for a return – that is, out of love – is able to receive according to the practices of giving out of love.

Further to the point of inter-subjectivity, Marion asks *a new question*: when someone gives himself through loving, it is, in fact, "a beloved who gives himself to another loved one." From the problem of inter-subjectivity, one moves to the problem of "reciprocal love." In fact, Marion believes that the inter-giving of love can open the way for the solution of the problem of "individualization of the others" (a problem which ethics, in the line of Levinas, would be unable to solve, since its focus would only be on the individualization of the responsible subject who discovers its uniqueness as an individual, therefore unrepeatable, precisely in virtue of the beckoning of the other's countenance who addresses him). How can he then reach others in his irreplaceable particularity? The response given by Marion carries the name of "love." And he believes that only a phenomenology of donation (a radically new one, therefore *agape*) might be able to give back to love "the dignity of a concept" (ivi, p. 395), thus paving the way for also a correct individualization of others.

Another important author of contemporary social theory, Axel Honneth, looks at love as being an important process for the formation of subjectivity. Being an exponent of the younger generation of "critical theory," he presents in 'The Struggle for Recognition' (Honneth, 1993), the features of a research program, which, in the Frankfurt tradition, proposes to put together sociological requirements (a better interpretation of social conflict) and elements of moral theory (models for recognition as a normative basis of relationships with yourself and others). The overall goals of this program are, in terms of social theory, to provide a unified account of the notions of social conflict and moral progress in the transition to cultural modernity, and in terms of moral theory, to outline a formal theory of the good life capable of avoiding interpretations that would be too demanding, from the moral point of view, but at the same time, without getting trapped in ethical details. The positive modalities of relationship with oneself – self-confidence, self-respect, self-esteem – are identified starting from the negative experiences of contempt, disrespect, humiliation, in turn understood as violations of the network of inter-subjective recognitions that support individual self-fulfillment. Individual integrity and social integration thus form a 'continuum' that, in Honneth's perspective, aims to delimit the axiological horizon of a post-traditional and democratic ethos.

In the quoted text, Honneth proposes three forms of recognition, which can be interpreted in a decreasing order: love, justice and solidarity. Honneth considers love as being all interpersonal relationships based on sympathy, unconditional acceptance and letting go of keeping track, which represent forms of approval and encouragement aimed at promoting ways of doing devoid of anxiety in relationship with themselves and with others, giving people the ability to stay all by themselves without fear; that is, to realize their autonomy by rejecting the symbiotic dependence on the other and the blaming derived from absolutist definitions of identity. Love, among other things, enables one to recognize the role of our relationship with the 'other,' a role that is constitutive of our identity and of our constant indebtedness to the 'other.'

Honneth's argument has theoretical ancient roots. In fact, he points out how in his youthful writings Hegel developed a model that makes use of social categories while, at the same time, giving ample room to the issue of inter-subjectivity. Quoting the Jenesian writings, Honneth recalls that in the struggle for life and death, there is the mutual recognition of one's own finitude and the realization of the awareness of the existential community founded on the limit, based on which, subjects learn to see themselves as being mutually vulnerable and threatened. Following this path, Honneth points out the common elements between Hegelian philosophy and the microsociology of George Herbert Mead. The latter is considered by Honneth as the post-metaphysical thinker who made the intersubjective Hegelian recognition no longer a transcendental issue, but a social one. He showed how the subject, since its appearance in the world, is in need of constant and secure relations as well as of an environment, which, as Winnicott says, is "good enough" to recognize itself as being transcendental and to be acknowledged as a person.

Recognizing the relationship with the other as being constitutive of one's own being and of one's own identity means that self-fulfillment cannot be separated from the other's self-fulfillment, that one's own proper autonomy cannot be promoted without promoting the other's autonomy. So, when my identity is built against the other's, in principle I am working against my own identity, as much as I tend to destroy the chance to see it recognized by the other.

To illustrate this dynamic, typically 'agapic' because it overflows, I consider it useful to return to the research done by post-Freudian psychoanalysis and, in particular, to the work of Winnicott on the conditions for a satisfactory socialization of children, in the context of a consideration of the behavioral mental disorders (Winnicott, 1970). These studies distance themselves from the original idea of Freud, according to which personality conflicts find their origins in intra-psychic events, to introduce instead interpersonal relational elements in the development of children's instinctual life (Eagle, 1993). Within this new conceptual framework, psychoanalysis broadens its horizons to social interactions, through which the child matures by learning to perceive himself as a subject gifted with his own autonomy. With these conceptual tools we can express our thesis that, along an uphill struggle for the affirmation of his own autonomy, the child (as well as every subject) can assert a non-anxious personality only if he is experiencing a relationship which we call love-*agape*.

Winnicott explains that during the first months of his life, the child and his mother live a symbiotic unity. On one hand, the child expresses a status of omnipotence, as he perceives maternal care as a result of his own will. On the other hand, the mother perceives the child's responses as an understanding which is part of a single action cycle. This undifferentiated relationship that is experienced by both was the basis of the question that prompted Winnicott's research, who wanted to search for the ways in which mother and child manage to get out from a state of indistinct unity to learn to accept one another and live as people who are different from each other. In other words, Winnicott is interested in studying the evolution of the mutual learning process that takes both subjects from a symbiotic unity to differentiate themselves into distinct and different beings who are not distressed by separation. The object of inquiry is then the mother-child inter-subjective relationship, which alone can indicate to us the development of a psychologically healthy personality.

Winnicott describes two phases of this relationship. The first phase is defined by the 'absolute dependence' category in which the two partners are fused in one another in the satisfaction of their needs, without anyone being able to draw a boundary between her/himself and the other. In fact, the mother perceives the newborn as absolutely helpless, but at the same time experiences in a projective manner her powerlessness. The infant, on the other hand – while not being able to express his physical and emotional needs – receives his experience of the world as mediated to him by the physical space of being 'held in the arms' of his mother.

This phase of mutual dependency ends only when both parties acquire room for their own autonomy. For the mother the opportunity comes in her return to the daily routine, which facilitates the separation from her child for progressively longer periods. For the newborn, this is the time for greater cognitive development, and the beginning of differentiation between the ego and the environment. The second phase starts around six months of age, when the baby starts for the first time to perceive the mother as being part of the outside world, not subject to his omnipotent and delusional control. For the first time, the child perceives its own dependent state, which Winnicott defines as 'relative dependency' (ibid., p. 103), an age that is decisive in the development of children's ability to build relationships. For Winnicott, this period of 'relative dependency' allows one to understand the foundational skills of a subject's personality.

During this stage the baby understands that the mother is no

longer at his omnipotent disposal and undergoes a process of disillusionment because he loses the subjective certainty of his focal
point of strength and presence in the world (Winnicott, 1997, pp.151-
164). The child may arrive at this stage through a very complex
psychological process that Winnicott describes through two mechanisms: the first one, on which we shall focus longer than the second one, is defined as 'destruction'; that is, a time of struggle and
conflict with the mother. The second one regards his concept of
'transitional phenomena.' In fact, the baby tends to rebel against
the mother's autonomy through behavioral conflicts that tend to
destroy the mother's body; by beating her, biting her, punching her,
or by sudden inconsolable crying which is a result of frustration.
Such a struggling behavior is the result of the loss of omnipotent
control on the child's part. These actions are, however, laden with
meaning, because the fact that the mother continues to exist – despite the baby's attacks – allows the baby to positively note that she
has an independent existence. This also helps the child to recognize
not only the mother as a being having her own autonomy, but that
there are also other people who have this characteristic. Such a process comes to fruition if the mother is able to love the child and not
respond in an equal manner to his violent behavior. It is only thanks
to this non-violent response by the mother that the child is able to
accept his dependent condition without succumbing to symbiotic
trends, and accept at the same time the mother's independence.

This phase also means that the mother must accept, on one hand,
a progressive independence of the child and, on the other hand, re-
sist his violent provocations. The mother, therefore, must be able to
behave in an overabundant manner, typical of love-*agape*. Only in
this process can a first step be taken towards reciprocal separation,
where each one can recognize himself / herself without the need to
merge symbiotically with the other, but as a different and distinct
person.

Our hermeneutic reinterpretation of Winnicott's research shows
us then that love-*agape* is central to the child's ability to perceive
itself as a subject with its own autonomy, not anxious and able in
his own turn to experience affection and love. If the mother is able
to pass the unconscious test of her child and does not take revenge
for his aggressive attacks by denying him love, then only in this case
will the child gain confidence in the possibility that his own requirements are met by the social context to which he belongs. Through
this process are laid the foundations for the subject to have the abil-

ity to be alone with himself without anxiety, to become aware of his inner impulses and be open to experience the world without fear of being lost in solitude. To sum up, the child absorbs the fact, while internalizing it, that the person who loves him still loves him even when she does not directs her attention towards him. When this process does not have positive outcomes, we find personalities marked by sadism and masochism, which are two clinical processes that characterize the subjects' personalities and express the failure of the first love relationship, which can be such only in its agapic declension.

According to Honneth, this relationship is the archetype of every love relationship. The last member of the Frankfurt School writes that mature love makes it possible to break the symbiosis, build mutual identification and be the foundation for participation in public life: "If love represents a broken symbiosis ... the loved one maintains her affection even after regaining her independence ... it illustrates the dual process by which the other person gains her freedom and at the same time consolidates an emotional bond" (Honneth, op. cit., p.131). In yet another passage, he brings into light the relevance of the love relationship: "The experience of being loved represents for each subject a necessary prerequisite to participate in the public life of a community" (ibid., p.51 ).

Through Winnicott's research, reinterpreted from the perspective of *agape*, it can be seen that conflict, struggle and aversion are within the dynamics of love-*agape*, and that when these two processes come together, they represent the inter-subjective conditions to which we must necessarily refer if we wish to describe the general structure of a good social life.

Marion, Honneth, Winnicott, i.e. a philosopher, a social theorist and a psychologist, show us how love, in its typical agapic form, which is identified by overabundance, an overflow, is a very contemporary theme to the subject and to the possibility of inter-subjectivity.

# 4.2 Genealogy of the West

For a historical sociology that uses the concept of *agape*, there are interesting ideas which come from the research of Arpad Szakolczai, presented in *Sociology, Religion and Grace* (2007a, 2007b). In particular, within this paragraph we re-visit, while reinterpreting it, the concept of grace as a fulcrum for the comparative-historical analysis of the origin and transformation of the Western world. This concept is analyzed, from our point of view, as love-*agape*.

Indeed *agape*, from the point of view of the recipient, presents itself as 'grace.' Should we follow the sense it can take in the various Indo-European languages, the word grace has an obvious relationship with love, because the Greek word *charis*, which is also love, love as *agape*, is the basis of the various meanings of grace. From the semantic point of view, therefore, we have three dimensions of the meaning of grace which we understand as specifications of *agape*. The first meaning is the theological one and expresses the bond of divine grace that is God's actions and its consequences. The second meaning covers the aesthetic dimension, understood as the beauty of a shape, of a movement or even of a behavior. It has thus an overall sense of graciousness. The third way concerns the semantic link with the social life and its pleasures, which generates feelings of gratitude and which expresses itself by saying 'thank you' for something received. We can therefore say that there are three aspects of grace: a 'religious' one, an 'aesthetic' one and a 'social' one.

If from linguistic analysis one moves to the historical level, through a crossing of the different meanings we can identify two particularly useful social configurations. In fact, on one hand we have the monotheistic religions (Judaism, Christianity and Islam) that bring together the theological and social meanings (grace and gratitude) and, on the other hand, the Hellenic culture that is identified by the aesthetic dimension and social ties (graciousness and gratitude).

These two components, the monotheistic religions and Greek civilization, represent for Szakolczai the foundations of the Western world.

### A. Judaism.

As it is by now accepted within scientific debate, Abraham is considered to be a contemporary of Hammurabi. Consequently the Jewish religion emerged during the first absolutist and bureaucratic empires at the beginning of the second millennium BC. Abraham's search of the Absolute and God's 'call' can be explained as a sensible refusal of that 'contemporary' civilization. Max Weber pointed out that the typical feature of monotheistic religions is the 'rejection of the world' (Weber, 2010). The world is to be understood as all those relationships that are beyond domestic ones, and therefore the refusal applies to all relationships of reciprocity which are asymmetrical relationships of power. The world, however, views empires, courts and kingdoms as characterized by asymmetrical relationships of reciprocity, where the latter presents itself under the light of abuse. Therefore, the main division is between 'home' and 'world.' The two poles express social historical dynamics which, in the evolutionary perspective sees the emergence of the 'logic of the world' over the 'domestic logic' (Elias, 1988).

From the historical point of view, this assumption is expressed by the departure of Abraham from Babylon and of Moses from Egypt. If in fact, as we have said it, Abraham is considered to be a contemporary of Hammurabi, this means that Judaism emerged in a context in which absolute empires were already in existence. The Code of Hammurabi is considered to be the ultimate expression of that novelty within antiquity. In such a context, Abraham's experience of God, his "divine call," can be interpreted along this sense as being a rejection of the civilization he found himself in.

For the religions of grace, the latter is linked to the possibility of being able to rise above the logic of the world. Abraham's experience (Voegelin, 1956) takes on the meaning of a conversion that is expressed through the distancing from the center of the 'society of courts' of that time, via the departure from Babylon. The purpose of the flight is to reform a new-old social structure in which asymmetrical relationships could dominate the whole of community life. The laws of Moses, on the other hand, are nothing more than a legalized attempt to set up the possibility of a new way of living.

### B. Greece.

Along this line of interpretation, according to Weber it is necessary to analyze the Greek case, which is particularly important in reference to mythology, history, politics and the fact that the Greek word *charis* is the basis of all the Indo-European terms related to the various meanings of grace. The origin of Greek culture has always been a headache for the giants of Western thought, starting from Plato to Hölderlin and Nietzsche. Szackolczai builds up and documents the thesis that Greek culture, and specifically the Athenian one, descends directly from the Minoan civilization of ancient Crete, which was destroyed around 1400 BC. The distinctiveness of this civilization is that it was generated by an 'experience-meeting' transcending towards a female figure, in contrast with the Jewish historical experience. For this reason it has been theorized within the myth of the 'abduction of Europe.'

The experience of meeting between men and women is radically different. The experience of a male prophet is characterized by a spiritual-intellectual level which emphasizes words, rationality, and leads to the establishment of a religion made up of ethical commandments, oriented towards the organization and conduct of life. The experience of a feminine encounter with the divine is completely different, as it is characterized by images more than by the word. It is less spiritualistic and more ascetic, and is characterized by an intimate and emotional lived experience, rather than being policy. It underlines sociability, which is the dimension of mutual gratitude in human relationships (Simmel, 1997).

From this point of view, one can understand why Christianity is not just a union between the Jewish religion and Greek culture, but rather the original and unprecedented meeting between the two great lines of originating transcendental meaning: the one associated with Abraham, the Jew, and the one associated with Europe, the Cretan-Minoan. The foundation of Christianity, therefore, is given by the synthesis of male Jewish roots and feminine Greek roots.

### C. Christianity and its novelty.

The novelty of Christianity is represented by the grace-*agape* that is, by the unexpected and gratuitous love of God, a true and absolute gift. This grace-*agape*, from the point of view of a comprehensive sociology, is given through the events of the Incarnation, the Cross and the Resurrection, which have put at the center of the religious experience the theme of the 'motivation of God.'

This emphasis, which is still marginal in the Gospels of Matthew and Mark, because they are closer to a Jewish reconstruction, is mostly present in the more 'Greek' reconstructions of Luke and especially John. The motivation of God has received an original formulation precisely in the concept of *agape* (Jn 3, 16, 1 Jn 4, 8:16). Love-*agape* is a word that characterizes Greek thinking in a much more emphatic manner than in the Jewish one. However, the keyword to express love for the Greeks is 'eros,' while in the New Testament we find the word *agape*, which is very marginal in the classical Greek language. This novelty is highlighted and underlined also by the Latin version, which translates *agape* not with love, but with another marginal word from the lexicon dating from the Romans, which is caritas. This choice underscores the difference in era between ancient thinking (Greco-Roman) and the Christian one.

Christianity's novelty lies in divine love that is revealed to humans through grace, that is, the idea of *agape*, which takes on the sense of absolute, transcendent and indifference not conditioned by the merits of each; that is, a universal sense. From the sociological point of view, then, the issue is the human consequences of a conception of God as *agape*, that is, people's responding interactions to the love-*agape* of God, or better, how humans behave with respect to the undeserved grace received, because it is beyond their own merits.

This element of the answer to this unconditional and universal love manifests itself in the search to improve oneself up the point of responding to the measure of grace: this response is the typical element of Christianity which we find neither in Judaism nor in Islam at its beginnings, nor in Greek philosophy, unless in a marginal manner. In fact, in ancient Judaism the need to maintain the Mosaic Law was underscored. Even in Islam any idea of working on the Self – in order to achieve a gradual perfection of one's way of life – was absent, in the sense of a philosophical ethos. In Greek culture the situation was not much different from the experiences we mentioned, because it lacked the vigor to make a change towards an improvement, except for a small group of members of a school of philosophy who in general practised *parrhesia* (Foucault, 1996).

From the point of view of human consequences and the work of improvement up to the 'care of the Self', the figure of Augustine of Hippo is of crucial importance in the history of Christianity and the Western world. As pointed out by Nygren (1971), in fact in his polemics against Pelagianism, Augustine sanctioned the divine heedlessness towards the merits of each and the gratuity of grace, which is a premise to the undertaking of a journey of personal perfection as an appropriate response to the invitation on the part of *agape*. As pointed out by Nygren, the concept of charity as per Augustine is even more important for the idea of an endeavor of self-improvement, a concept which is a synthesis of *agape* and eros. In Greek philosophy, and especially for Plato, eros was about love in its sexual form, but it also indicated a spiritual level of requirement of unity of the soul with God (the One). The Platonic eros, therefore, was about a self-love based on the desire to unite oneself with what is different, in order to recompose a fuller unity. In Christianity, the novelty is the love-*agape* coming down from God towards human beings without making reference to particular merits, a love marked by not keeping track of what is given and received. For Augustine *caritas* is the unity between these two dimensions of love and, therefore, when the human person is touched by the grace of *agape*, s/he must respond with a conversion translated into daily and concrete acts (eros) that results in unity with her/his neighbor. The synthesis that Augustine developed is also the product of his sociological condition as a man who lived between two worlds: the world of antiquity and the early Middle Ages. Not by chance did Augustine die during the siege of Carthage by the Vandals, who un-equivocally marked the passing of an era.

### The three dimensions of *agape* in history: the dialectic between Renaissance and Reformation.

The three dimensions of what we called grace-*agape* – while rein-terpreting Szackolczai (and continuing along his line of analysis) – historically mingle, giving life to the dialectic between 'Renaissance' and 'Reformation.' Rebirths are about the new blooming of culture and art, and consequently have a feminine tone. They arise from reforms that appeal to a more authentic evangelical life, and to a radical rejection of the world. Therefore, they also have a masculine intonation.

For Szackolczai the thirteenth century represented for humanity a promise that was denied by modernity, in which European Chris-tian culture developed a novel synthesis between the three dimen-sions of grace-agape through Franciscanhumanism. This culture found its best expression in the Higher Renaissance, between the late fifteenth and early sixteenth centuries. During those years Leonardo, Michelangelo and Raphael produced their works. It is no coincidence that Franciscanism became the first "school" of eco-nomics from which emerged the modern spirit of a market econ-omy, and the movement from which emerged the first banks, the pawnshops, which were true forerunners of modern micro-credit. In fact, we find the first systematic reflections about economy, the value and price of goods or of currency, in the works of William of Ockam, Pietro Giovanni Olivi, Duns Scoto, all of whom are Francis-can thinkers (Bruni, 2010). Thus, the theological, artistic and so-cial dimensions of grace-*agape* find a perfect synthesis, each with its specific own weighting, a synthesis that to our days remains un-equaled.

The social configuration that took shape during the thirteenth cen-tury started to go off track and enter into crisis during the fifteenth century, that is, at the apex of its expression. This happened in the first place because of the emergence of a philosophical movement that placed great emphasis on the quest for a formal perfection of thought. This was the main objective of Ficino and Pico della Mirandola, who revisited, while taking it to the extremes, the analysis of Plato's theses, leading *de facto* to a deification of the human being, with all its consequences on the social level.

On the historical level, a further element of crisis was brought about by the papal issue. In particular, the most important aspect was about the return of the papacy to Rome with the Council of Constance, which represented a crucial event for Europe, a return that was wanted for religious and devotional reasons. The formation of a new power center set the conditions for a new 'society of courts' (Elias, 1987). A particularly significant aspect was the phenomenon of *Il Momo*, as described by Leon Battista Alberti, who starting from 1436 was adviser to Pope Eugene IV – heir of Martin V – and acknowledged the formation of an individual who thrives on division, creates conflicts and sows discord. In fact, his place is precisely life in court.

These are the elements which underline the end of the synthesis of the thirteenth century and lay down the basis of modernity, and its crisis in our times. In the High Renaissance were born the three protagonists of art and culture who created archetypal figures of the modern individual. They were Leonardo with the 'Doubting Thomas,' Michelangelo with the figure of 'David,' and Raphael with the representation of the 'Marian Clairvoyant.' It was especially the first two who had an extraordinary influence, proposing the idea of a divided personality, put down by obligations and agonizing uncertainties destined to remain unsolved, always in doubt and lacking faith in one's neighbour. Should we add to the protagonists of figurative art the leading thinking figures of those times, such as Machiavelli, Thomas Moore and Luther, who worked at the beginning of the sixteenth century on their most important works (The Prince, Utopia and the Letter of Saint Paul to the Romans), one can underline the decisive breakdown and fragmentation of the three aspects of *agape*-grace. This incompatibility is what still today anguishes the individual and contemporary society, that is, the definitive separation between the theological grace-*agape*, as expressed in the predestination doctrine of the Lutheran Reformation; the aesthetic grace-*agape* as expressed by the affectation of the 'society of courts' in the first place, and, later on, by the aestheticism and anti-aestheticism of modern art; and social grace-*agape* as expressed by the theme of charity and organized by voluntary associations to help the poor and the dispossessed, which then turned into institutional and disciplinary mechanisms of the modern State.

These three aspects are well expressed in their degeneration and divergences in the analyses of the essence of modernity by three giants of modern social thought, namely Max Weber in *The Protestant Ethic and the Spirit of Capitalism* (2010), Norbert Elias in *The Process of Civilization* (1988) and Michel Foucault in *Discipline and Punish* (1988). This reflection leads one to wonder about the causes of failure and the dynamics of its development, which seemed to be irreversible in some respects, but also to encourage a vision capable of viewing the eventual consolidation of the three roots of *agape* as grace, within the crisis of modernity in its Western version, starting from its genealogical reconstruction.

# 4.3 Conclusion

In this chapter we have seen how *agape* is a dimension that is present in social relationships. In particular, using Winnicott's post-Freudian research on the mother-child relationship, we were able to show that only an overabundant behavior on the mother's part makes it to break the symbiosis and lay the foundations for an individualized non-anxious personality, which enables one to be alone with himself and build the foundations for public participation.

However, we have seen how agapic love empirically transforms the object and the loving subject as well, such as the mother who is no longer the same after having loved. The philosopher Marion, on his part, shows that the subject is such in so far as he is subjugated, meaning he is a subject, as he is loved by someone first, the only element that finds a solution to the problem of intersubjectivity, that is, to the possibility of access to the other insofar as he is other, without remaining closed solipsistically in himself. Then, the topic of 'individualization of the other' would resolve itself in loving, the only way capable of making us meet the other in his otherness, meaning to give, because each one is a subjugated being. On this point even Honneth notices that love is that experience that allows us to build our own radical difference, which is reproduced in the recognition of the vulnerability of human existence.

At the macro level, however, using the reflections of Szakolczai on the origins of modernity, we have shown that *agape* is a hermeneutic concept that, with a long-term vision, allows us to reach a double interpretation, a genealogical one as well as that of the crisis of modernity.

Chapter 5

# Case Studies

In this chapter we want to look at case studies in which highlighting the surplus in *agape* allows us to interpret actions that otherwise would lend themselves to a merely moral analysis. Three cases will be presented. Two of them concern individuals who in war situations and maximum human humiliation found the strength to be overabundant in their behavior, breaking down the reciprocity of violence and degradation. One case, however, is about a social movement, that of free software, which in its operating logic expresses an ethical behavior which is also based on overabundance and on action that eliminates keeping track of what is given and received.

## 5.1 Perlasca

The biography of a man present in the Court of the Righteous in Jerusalem leads us to the theme of the anomaly which exists in the phenomenology of the social. "What would you have done in my place?" was Giorgio Perlasca's response to the interviewer, after having been recognized in 1989 as a "righteous man" in Hungary, Israel, USA, Spain and, finally, also in Italy. In 1944, during the winter of Budapest, he managed to save thousands of people from the genocide, the vast majority of whom were Jews. He – a Fascist militant and a volunteer for Franco, Spain's dictator, a non-practicing Catholic, who loved the pleasures of life, a merchant – passed off as the Spanish consul after the ambassador's sudden flight, given the deterioration of the situation, providing protection to more than five thousand people. Entangled in the chaotic end of the Second World War, in an unknown country, with no official papers or money, instead of thinking of saving his life, he remained in a dangerous situation. His action did not stop at a single gesture, but lasted months. He had no role but created it. He was no fool and showed great organizational skills, which yielded unexpected results in very risky conditions. Then, after the end of the war, he went back home, living in an oblivion that lasted nearly half a century, during which he tried to remind himself of facts, places, and circumstances, as if to keep memories alive and check the coherence of his life experience. When he tried to communicate his "deeds," he felt he was perceived as being an exalted person by those who listened to him. Then the discovery came about – after the oblivion. It was not through his putting himself in the media or institutional limelight, but a group of women – young girls at the time when those events took place in Hungary - who owed him their lives and who wanted to remember, testify, show gratitude and give thanks, who did it (Deaglio, 2009).

In addition, the case of Perlasca is perfect to express the difference between *agape* and solidarity. He was a man who was alone. For some, he could have been an imposter. He could have escaped but did not do so. He could have safeguarded his own life, but instead ran the risk of being killed in order to carry out a duty that he felt so strongly. He had not money but nevertheless found the means to feed thousands of people. Every day he went to the station to disembark people from the trains who were being sent to the concentration camps by showing false Spanish documents that he himself had printed. He had no friend to whom to reveal his true identity as an Italian; no one knew that he was not a diplomat, no one knew that he was a fugitive. Therefore, he did not practice solidarity, for the reasons we highlighted, a conceptual category able to express the typical nature of an action such as Perlasca's. He did not share the values of a community to which he belonged, he did not collaborate with others and his actions were not done in conjunction with anyone else. Furthermore, he had no set area defined by a group that he belonged to for his social actions, nor did he express a behavior that was guided by shared regulations, both with respect to the belligerent and the neutral nations. In fact, no one could appreciate his actions: he did not have reciprocity or symmetry with anyone in what he was doing, since it could cost him his life.

"What would you have done in my place?" The question is embarrassing for the interviewer who asked him "why?". But how can we explain it on a sociological level?

Compared with the five dimensions of *agape*, we find that Perlasca definitely is a figure that expresses a maximum **intensity** of *agape*, because he risks his own life to protect the lives of Hungarian Jews during the Second World War.

**Extension**: Even with respect to this dimension Perlasca shows the highest level because he is a Catholic and helps Jews. He is a non-practicing person and cares for devout people, he could escape and instead remains, is in danger and does not protect himself, is a Fascist and goes against the official thinking of his reference group, is an Italian and helps Hungarians. Mostly, his action makes no distinction regarding the characteristics of those he encounters. So, his love-*agape*, in that context, reaches its maximum extent.

*Duration*: Perlasca's love-*agape* is limited in time. He is not a saint; he is a hero during the time required to achieve the objectives he had assigned himself. And then his life, as he himself says, is studded with vices. His overabundant behavior lasts as long as his encounter with the terrified faces of the fugitives.

*Purity*: For Perlasca there is purity in as much as his behavior is almost instinctive, unreflective. In fact, the question: "What would have done in my place?" expresses naturalness and an absence of a project thought through in a cognitive manner. He believes that anyone in his place would have done the same thing, so no one should repay him for what he has done.

*Adequacy*: In the case of Perlasca, we can observe a high level of mismatch between his intentions and attitudes, which are not consciously agapic, and his overabundant behavior that makes it objectively effective in saving lives and offers benefits without any possibility of payback: the forgetfulness of his actions lasted about forty years.

## 5.2 Peer-to-Peer

Peer-to-Peer, whose acronym is P2P, i.e. 'on equal terms,' means in itself a configuration between computers, but it also is a commercial logic, an innovation strategy, a social model driven by values and norms that orient social action with agapic traces. We use traces in the sense of what happened, of small quantities, of residues. But it can also be understood as a preparatory draft of a possible configuration. In its early phase, Internet was totally 'on equal terms,' that is, every computer had the same role with respect to the other. In this way each computer made available to the others its possessions, data, information, usage, etc. In those days there were a limited number of computers (hosts) connected to each other and everyone made available its resources, that is, each node was equipped with an FTP system to allow other peers to upload files in their memory or download from it.

Various versions of P2P software were circulating. Those who made history definitely are: Napster, Gnutella and Freenet. Napster was conveyed by Gene Kahn who used the happy metaphor of a party. A Client goes to a party. He knows the host, Server, but the other guests are totally unknown to him. Addressing Server, the Client asks him whether among those present there is someone who can give him the recipe for the Viennese *Sacher Torte*. Meanwhile, the Client tells Server about his knowledge in astrophysics. Server thinks about it for a bit and indicates to him that Tom at table 3, Dick at table 7 and Harry at table 38 have the recipe. Client gets in touch with them and gets the recipe by downloading it. This is the logic of the technical Client/ Server model, which has been transformed into P2P by the young Shawn Fanning, who is Napster's creator for the direct exchange of music, movies and software in general, Napster being the forerunner of the shareware sites.

Gnutella is another highly decentralized P2P system. In fact, there are different Servers that self-invite themselves to the Gnutella Club, according to the logic that each one is free to invite others. In this case, Tom was invited by Dick, whom he asks: "Do you know the recipe for *Sacher Torte*?" At this point, Dick sends out the question to the people who are physically present until someone gives him a positive answer, from whom Dick makes the download.

Freenet is the most radical expression of free and progressive software, invented by Ian Clarke, a young student in Edinburgh. Its objective is to ensure freedom of expression through absolute anonymity and to prevent, therefore, any censorship. As in the case of Gnutella, there is no central server with respect to others for any inbound, outbound or coordinating function. As in the case of Gnutella, the request for a document or information is forwarded to the present servers. It proceeds along the chain until it finds the initial answer. At this point the answer goes back on the tracks of the inquiry, so that each server hosts on its own node the document containing the request, but not its content.

Other P2P software programs have the same objective of protecting freedom of expression, anonymity and dissemination. Some examples are Publius, created by young people such as Marc Waldman, Lorrie Faith Cranor and Avi Rubin. Free Haven, designed and created by young people such as Michael Freedman from MIT and David Molnar from Harvard.

The 'peer-to-peer,' therefore, is not only a configuration among machines, but a concept of social relations. Those who support this logic believe that one goes online to 'put in common' requirements, needs and talents of each one to form a 'common good' from which everyone can draw. That was a capital that grew incrementally according to the logic of 'give and you shall receive,' a co-operative one, which was at the basis of the Internet in its early days, and of the best story of social and technological innovation.

But the paradigmatic case is Linux.

> A: newsgroup os.comp.minix.
> From: torvalds@klaava.Helsinki.FI (Linus Benedict Torvalds)
> "I am working on a small operating system for my 386 computer. I started working on it as a hobby in April, and now it is almost ready ... I would love to know what you think, whether you have any suggestions."

It was on August 25, 1991 that Linus Torvalds sent this message to the Usenet discussion group dedicated to the operating system Mimix. This post was noticed by Ari Lemke from the University of Helsinki who provided him, free of charge, with some disk space on the department's Internet server. The incubator of its development was at: ftp.funet.fi

Linux would have never seen the light without the free of charge network pooling of resources. Without this personal emptying, it would not have been possible to create this common room of added value. Torvald was in Finland and, thanks to the net, he could receive advice, criticisms and contributions. Each one donated, in an overabundant manner, everything of himself in order to offer support without keeping track of what was given and received, in order to achieve the common goal.

Linus gave back because he first received: to get a software that would work he drew on solutions that were already available on the net, solutions which were mostly restricted to a special software license called GPL (Gnu Public License). The license allows one to take original programs and modify them, but he has the obligation to make the results public. Everyone agrees not to sell on his own, nor to patent or make a profit from software products, including pieces covered by GPL. And so, the fact of having received produces only more common goods. Linus, therefore, could have never finished the new operating system on his own because he would not have had the wherewithal to write so much software covered by the agapic logic.

It was Richard Stallman, a programmer at the Massachusetts Institute of Technology (MIT), who gave life to the Free Software Foundation, which aims to produce and distribute software not subject to property rights. Stallman is the creator of the GPL license and of Copyleft, which is different from Copyright. The free circulation of resources, according to an agapic logic, takes on a legal obligation which aims at ensuring the freedom of distributing copies of free software and receiving the source code, changing it and using parts in other programs. This means that programmer A creates software and makes known the source program, accompanied by the statement that it is GPL software. Programmer B can see it, study it, examine it, use it, change it and insert it in other programs he created. But when he publishes his programs, he must submit them to the GPL regime. In this way the freedom of production, distribution and storage of software become jointly owned by allowing each one the freedom to use them over time and space. There is a constraint in this case, but is a constraint to reproduce an action process based on giving with no strings attached, free from any obligation to reciprocate what was received. This link is transmitted in the future, to children and grandchildren, because it is inalienable.

By the end of 2001 Linux became a complete operating system, in working order and especially adaptable to the user's needs. It can be used to run portable terminals, such as mobile phones and PDAs, or to operate a personal computer, or even for large mainframe computers. Linux is used by individuals for both profit and non-profit purposes, e.g. universities, public administrations, as well as publicly listed companies. In October 2001, the e-commerce giant Amazon.com stated in its financial statements filed with the SEC of Wall Street that it had reduced its technology expenses by 25 percent (from $71 to $54 million), and that much of the savings was attributable to the migration to a Linux-based platform. Even IBM and Cisco Systems migrated to Linux and Microsoft recently declared it would make public the code of its Windows proprietary system.

The logic of open source software has spread among many players. There are new open software programs such as Perl, Apache, Sendmail, to name the best known ones, which operate according to this overabundance logic, of free pooling of resources, solutions and experiences. Apache, for example, is a program that runs web pages, receiving requests coming from surfers and 'attending' to their requests. In technical terms, it is a web server. However, Apache operates because around it grew a community of developers and programmers who replay Linux's logic, in which a multitude of subjects

– let's call them software artisans – dedicate time, experience and professionalism in an agapic way to others or to the good that is put in common, meaning that each one has an overabundant behavior when compared with what the situation requires. The same can be said about Sendmail.

During the first half of the nineties, Tim Berners-Lee invented the World Wide Web. He worked out a code known as 'Hyper Text Markup Language,' better known by the acronym HTML, which in fact is a programming language. The HTML has spread and the Internet has become a reality, thanks to open and non-proprietary standards allowing numerous of people to make it their own, by imitation and copying. In addition to this element, one needs to underline two more factors. The first one concerns the fact that HTML is characterized by openness and universality because from its very beginnings, it was an invention given with no strings attached. The second element of its diffusion is connected to the desire to 'speak up,' because anyone with a computer could make his/her personal page.

The same is possible with two other technical artifacts (or ideas translated in code), which, freely given to the community by software writers, allow for the enrichment of web pages and, consequently, communication opportunities: programming in JavaScript and the Style Sheet. For example, the first one allows one to move a cursor over an image and change it, while the latter is used to manage the font characteristics of one or more web pages. These programs were created and offered with free access to the source code, so they can be freely examined and modified. Therefore everyone can make functional changes and make them available to the community, multiplying in an exponential manner its diffusion and innovative dynamics.

Among the projects linked to a logic of agapic overabundance, a noteworthy one is Open directory. It is one of shared knowledge projects that stimulate the Web. Its characteristic lies in the sharing of knowledge resources. Open Directory is an ordered list of sites, in which people review sites and create true and real search engines. As in the case of Yahoo! the review of sites, their selection and description are entrusted to people and not to automated software systems. The difference lies in the fact that those of Yahoo are employees of a commercial enterprise, which in early 2002 had a market capitalization of $ 10 billion, while the Open Directory is a non-profit project of unpaid volunteer reviewers spread throughout the world. Anyone can become a reviewer, offering an agapic gesture to the network community.

The same logic of *agape* can be found in the mechanisms that drive the universal encyclopedia project called Wikipedia.com, which was born in 2001 thanks to Jimmy Wales of San Diego, California, who invested $ 150,000 of his savings, with no expectation of an economic return. During the first year of operations, he collected and proposed to the virtual community – to be read and commented – about 10,000 entries. Since then the project has spread out; the contents of the encyclopedia have grown because any person can write an entry about the topics in which s/he feels to be an expert. It is recommended to submit non-controversial and objective texts, while no supervision is done by a higher authority. The verification and correction controls are entrusted to readers, each of whom, entering into the agapic logic, can become a reviewer, corrector and an author in his own turn. In all these cases, it is assumed that people have things to say, that they are repositories of knowledge which they gladly and freely offer to others according to an agapic logic. Their only reward comes from being recognized as experts, to build for themselves a positive reputation.

In this respect, an interesting research was published by the journal *Nature* in December 2005, in which forty items from Wikipedia encyclopedia were compared to an equal number within the Britannica Encyclopedia. Findings showed that in the Wiki world there were about four errors compared with every three in Britannica. On the other hand, Wikipedia would be more precise in the definition of words. In fact, the two works are equivalent, but there is a mutation in the way of building, storing and transmitting knowledge. One is the product of a prestigious and contracted editorial staff, while the other one is dealing with the zealous culture of volunteers spread out all over the place (cited in Bartezzaghi, 2006).

What prompted Linus Torvalds to refuse to join the board of directors of a UK company that, to have him jump in, offered him $10 million dollars. What prompted Tim Berners Lee, inventor of the World Wide Web, not to patent the HTML language and to direct the non-profit W3C consortium? Who suggested to Jimmy Wales to invest money in his project of distributed knowledge and collective intelligence, without any economic pay-back?

We hypothesize that Torvalds, Tim and Jimmy are not only representative of a world-wide movement, but that they are the expression of an action that is not only non-instrumental, but that finds its identity because it is based on *agape*, that is, on an overabundant behavior, an excess with respect to what the contexts and subjects require in terms of data, bringing out the disposition of collective creativity, of generative capacity for this type of social action. But one should also point out that the logic of overabundant capacity, typical of *agape*, has the capability of becoming institutional, in the sense of being a bearer of values, norms, social roles and groups.

What does the movement Peer-to-Peer express with respect to our analytical dimensions?

***Intensity:*** the communities which have been analyzed are characterized by a high level of agapic intensity. In fact, involved put everything in common: their interests / requirements / solutions that become the pre-requisites for future advances in knowledge or technology. Linus precisely addressed a community of strangers:

> "I am working on a small operating system for my 386 computer. I started working on it as a hobby in April, and now it is almost ready ... I would love to know what you think, whether you have any suggestions."

Nothing stays confidential when asking or giving. Everyone becomes a 'loved one,' i.e. a subjectivity that is constituted as it has received benefits and, therefore, in turn responds in an overabundant manner, i.e. by offering more than the situation would require. By thus forgetting about keeping track of what has been received or given and how much the situation requires, each person builds relationships and subjectivities which are characterized by 'overabundant inter-giving ,' thus agapic type relationships.

Looking at things through such a vision, we find empirical support for the proposal that sees *agape* as a primary motivation. Egoism and altruism, therefore, are not the two extremes of the continuum of human motivation. Social action out of love is independent of that alternative. It eliminates the distance between the 'I' and the 'you.' In Simmel's words, the specific particularity of love is that:

> "... in itself it does not do away with the being of the I or with the you, but it rather makes of it the prerequisite based on which the distance is eliminated" (p.161).

Selfishness implies that there is an identity, and that situations are exploited in an instrumental manner by the subject in order to increase that individual identity. Altruism, however, presupposes that a person always acts on behalf of and in favor of others. Agape does not fall in any of the two categories, because on the one hand it presupposes them, and, on the other hand, constitutes them.

In the case of the free software community, stakeholders portray their action not so much for the selfish dimension, which is present in as much as they have, for example, the need to build a website using software written by others, not even for the altruistic dimension, because they are not interested in the fact of helping others as an end in itself. They are players who even in their unconsciousness love – in the sense that each one is able to do something, to write a piece of code, to add a function to a program, using the knowledge and offers (gifts) of previous acts of love and – each in turn contributes to creating the virtuous cycle of reciprocity of love, therefore an agapic way of doing things. In fact, what is the Internet that was invented by Berners Lee if not a putting together of earlier inventions such as digital archives, modems for data transmission via telephone and hypertext logic? As a recipient, Berners Lee – being a person who had received pre-existing gifts (digital archives, modems and hypertext) – added the HTML language and re-offered it to the community by triggering the mechanism of *agape*, and others, while being fully unaware (in the sense of the person who appears to us in the immediacy that is perceptible to our senses) of what has been received and how given. Berners-Lee could have become a billionaire by patenting his invention, but chose not to.

***Extension***: Even this aspect has an eminent value, because the participants in P2P are subjects who put in common with all members of the community, but also with outsiders, their possessions / knowledge / solutions / requirements. It is interesting to draw attention to the dimension of anonymity of those who receive compared to the one he loves. To the case of "dedication to a P2P community" whose members are unknown, or when one loves a category of individuals as a nation, a community of choice, children, students, donating time, energy and life. In this case, the beloved are not single tangible persons. These, on one hand, are not physically actually "present" to the lover (talking, in our case, of code donors) and, on the other hand, cannot accept the excess, the donation of software, code, if not to pass it on to future recipients.

In this case, one would then have concrete love in a second position – as if between brackets – and the opening of a horizon of a universal beloved, in which the gift can present *itself* in its phenomenological "perfect form": one gives without discriminating among people, with a complete indifference as to the merit or lack of merit of the loved person, while being fully unconcerned with any eventual reciprocity.

In this case, we reach the paradox that the gift, without a transcendent beloved, and then "in conformity with the donation," appears only to the donor, as its immanent lived consciousness. The donor then takes on the role of the beloved, and becomes the beneficiary: in fact, it is to him, a "phenomenological witness of the gift without concrete beloved," that the gift is about to appear. To sum up: "even without a beneficiary, *agape* fulfills *itself* because it is enough for it to give itself in order to manifest itself (to the lover)" (115).

**Duration**: along this dimension we can find different situations, among whoever is a builder or a mere user of P2P. Builders have a commitment in this field, which is more important than the role of simple users, as in the case of Wikipedia. He who writes an entry in the encyclopedia makes public certain knowledge that is the product of a long time of work and commitment. On the other hand, the users can be passive and what more manifest opportunistic behavior. P2P builders, however, are those who spend a lot of time, effort and willingness within their efforts to solve their own/other technical problems or knowledge issues. It is realistically conceivable, however, that the duration of this commitment will not always be along this agapic dimension, but that such behavior is linked to the spirit of functioning of the Net. Agape is unmindful of the past and the future. It is focused on the present moment, the only anchor to act without looking at what happened yesterday or will happen in the future, whether tomorrow the community will respond with appropriate solutions to one's request. Everything is forgetfulness or ignorance; this is why its temporal horizon has no limits, but as Kierkegaard pointed out, it has permanence, in the sense that action is present in every moment to itself, sheltered from trials. Given the fragmentation of the working time devoted to free software, we assign an intermediate value equal to 50.

**Purity**: To purity we attach a value next to the minimum. P2P does not come about, in the intents of the protagonists, to create agapic social realities, but certainly in its founders the movement had cooperative intentions and openly non-utilitarian ideals. Furthermore, many stakeholders work in it to obtain fame and credibility. Even more so, reputation is the prevailing currency of exchange among Internet users. Others, instead, while spreading benefits and solutions for the members of virtual communities, remain anonymous, as in the case of knowledge disseminated through Wikipedia. We can therefore estimate a minimum level of purity in P2P.

There is a need, however, to consider that the person in the state of *agape* – given that s/he is all projected in the present moment – is in a state of silence, of suspension of any judgment on her/his partner, and does not anticipate any action or speculation on how s/he will use that work. The makers of the free software movement do not care to know the motivations and purposes of those who use their software, because they are in a state of surplus. Agape, in fact, does not care about the motivations of those who receive, because it is sufficient to itself. Many Internet sites use free software for the most various goals, even for commercial use. The free software movement only requires that one mention the software which has been used to build the website. We can therefore say that through its action *agape* is foundational; it does not create disputes, but gains its authority through its acts. Freeing itself from any formalism, from the intention of judgment towards other people, it frees itself from any possible dispute. Agape has an internalized rule and its validity is established by the intent of love, and it does not prescribe anything to others. Because of this, it frees subjects from the anxiety that the other will return what has been received (proposition n. 5).

But then love holds within itself a *tragic* aspect (proposition n.3). Agape, in generating the other who is different from itself (by loving him) is a creative act that is unrelated or even opposed to the reality of he who created it (the reality of non-love). The tragic aspect of love, moreover, is just in its law, which is accomplished in generating the other 'different' self, what is alien or even opposed to him, especially with respect to the world in which he often does not find his place, but which has nonetheless attained the strength for its birth and preservation. In fact, within the Internet we find the most diverse realities: people use HTML to provoke terrorism, fuel violence and hatred, abuse of power, to do legitimate business or to spread scams. Everyone uses the Net's resources like cash (paraphrasing Simmel), using it according to one's purposes, even in order to sustain inhumanity.

**Adequacy** : In this case *agape* points to values close to zero as we are faced with situations that are definitely inadequate. The traces of *agape*, as found in the Open Source movement, P2P and file-sharing projects, are inadequate in the sense that the relationship between the subjective intention of love and its objective manifestations do not coincide. Consequently, we assign a value close to zero, i.e. equivalent to 5. The intentions of the leaders of the movement we examined are not based on an agapic action, but their effects are undoubtedly agapic, in the sense of surplus. And yet experiences such as Wikipedia, P2P sites, the Open Source movement did objectify, meaning they have become institutions in as much as they provide values, social norms and roles which require adequate behaviors and give life to interacting groups that share a common culture (propositions n. 2 and n. 7).

According to some of Marion's suggestions, this is the case of the *unawareness* of the lover, that is, when the one who is loved is unknown to oneself; the subject loves in a agapic manner without being conscious of or having the intention of love (surplus), thereby ignoring the "effect" that he provokes in others, the gratitude from which stems the fact of saying "thank you." Let us think of some comparable figures of software creators, of sportspersons or artists, who grant victory to a beloved one, or the aesthetic effect, often without knowing the scope or depth of what they stirred in the other person, or at least live the "gap" between what they experience and the effect they produce in other people. In fact, a law within the essence of *agape* is that in order to exceed and give, there is no need to know oneself as being the loving one, as per the saying of the Gospel: "When you give alms, do not let your left hand know what your right hand is doing" (Matthew 6:3). As a result, Marion speaks of the "paradox" between the ego of the donor, which is such the less it is aware of itself as donor. "The *ego is*, in as much as it returns identically to itself; the donor *is not* (is absent, vanishes, remains unknown, anonymous) in as much as he (*s/he*) gives himself or herself" (Marion, op. cit., p. 120).

Agape, therefore, transcends the action of the one who does it (proposition n. 4), in the sense that it creates a reality that is different from the previous one in which they were immersed either as Alter or as Ego, that is, before they acted out of love. The fate of the agapic action is burning behind itself the bridges it built for its own path, and to recognize in that same break its deepest need.

Agape transcends the reality of ordinary existence because it postulates, albeit temporarily and alongside other forms of action, a different reality in which the principles and the rules of everyday life are put on hold. This is an aspect of social transcendence, in as much as these manifestations of agapic action make one think that this 'other' reality has redemptive virtues which are not short-lived, and point towards that 'other world' that is always possible.

For example, Peter Berger, in the case of *Homo Ridens* speaks of a 'liberating' laughter to explain the transcendence of the comical, highlighting how it bursts in the consciousness of everyday reality that we share and which therefore comes out as being real. Every day life is a heavy reality, an irresistible one which imposes itself. The funny side is subtle, sometimes shared sometimes not. It is a ' limited sphere of meaning,' i.e. it is like an island within the ocean of daily experience, meaning it has distinct categories of space and time, different appreciations of reality, diverse experiences of its entry and exit borders, etc. (Berger, 1999, pp. 293-308).

*Agape* leads us to transcend everyday reality, because it is not routine, not a typical action, but, on the contrary, the subject is always ready to head towards new shores, new experiences that s/he who passes beside him can ask for. It has its own sensory features (space, time, confines, entry, exit, etc.) that are extraordinary when compared with daily routine.

In conclusion, we can show that a characteristic of this dimension of *agape* in the movement of P2P is the inadequacy and scarce purity, correlated to the limited duration.

## 5.3 Divjak: Political Resistance

Agape is radical and allows people who find themselves in situations of humiliation, suffering and disregard to judge only those who ignore rules and become outlaws, with respect to laws and common sense. For example, he who is shocked by persecution taking place in Moscow with respect to a political campaign against an enemy of the people, proves himself of capable of a reflective judgment. He assesses things based on reality and rediscovers within particular moral values that have been put aside. A revolutionary act thus takes place: a person judges by herself, without moral references, and is then capable through this overabundance to find again the general rules of life, adapting them to the whole world.

General Jovan Divjak has lived this kind of experience. He is the hero of the resistance of Sarajevo during the years of the city's siege, who from time to time, in facing unexpected situations freed himself from political constraints, from the recall of his nationality and the political correctness of a just cause,in giving back what had been received. Every time he had to form an opinion all by himself and rediscover moral laws, while never seeking an easy consensus. In the war situation in the former Yugoslavia, understanding on which side the perpetrators of ethnic cleansing were and the ones who were persecuted was not an easy daily endeavor. The situation was difficult, because there was not only one culprit, such as President Slobodan Milošević who tried to impose himself on other nationalities to give birth to the great Serbia, or all the persons responsible for the nationalities being attacked, who, in their own turn, had criminalized and persecuted their minorities. The one who underwent evil treatment and aggression was in his own turn involved in crimes against humanity. He asked for world solidarity for his just cause and then behaved towards others using the same methods of his aggressor. In such cases it is really difficult to find ways to reach an agreement, and then be forced to reject them.

Divjak was a staunch Communist. He studied the classics of Marxism and enrolled at the Military Academy in Belgrade. He loved Yugoslavia and the power of Stalin's Russia. He felt he was living in a promised land and that he knew the moral principles that govern the world. In fact, he found the country of goodness, the ideology that directed his life and the most coveted job that a graduate of the Military Academy can have in Belgrade. But everything changed when he was faced with the secessions of Slovenia and Croatia. It is not easy to guess in which direction history was going, who was right and who was wrong.

Divjak was torn apart: should he judge events based on his old moral criteria, he would then led to consider Serbia as a safeguard against the disintegration of the country. During the early months of the war, he sided with Milošević. Under orders from Belgrade, Divjak was the commander of the territorial defense of Sarajevo. When he became aware that Milošević had transformed the old multiethnic Yugoslav army into a military body directed by Belgrade, and that he fomented a Serbian secession in Bosnia, Jovan was confused and divided. He understood that the old communist and multiethnic Yugoslavia no longer existed and had to decide on his own what to do: return to Belgrade or live in a Sarajevo which would no longer be like before. He no longer had clear ideas, and tradition did not help him. He had to discern what is good and evil in things, no longer counting on ideological certainties, and paid a high price for it.

This scenario calls to mind the possibility of bringing about benefits, provided they are overabundant:

"I had been sent from Belgrade to Bosnia with the task of defending the cohesion of Yugoslavia, but I found myself defending the independence of Sarajevo; seeing the dead and the injustice, I changed my mind" (Nissim, 2011, p. 148).

This stance made him experience an unexpected loneliness. In order to defend truth he lost many of his friends. The multinational command was given up by almost all of the Serbian officers. Two-thirds of the army did not show up for the fight; the call of blood and of the families who live in Serbia is just too strong and they decided to leave Sarajevo. Bombs fell on the city and the Serbian artillery repeatedly shot on the city from positions of hiding on surrounding hills, killing the young people of a Muslim family. He, a Serbian, with some fear, decided to go visit the family. The mother of the murdered boys greets him: "Welcome commander!" They tell him they wanted to take revenge, take cans of gasoline and set fire to homes of Serb people. He listens to them and, keeping this attitude throughout the war, Jovan tried to prove that his origin does not matter and that he felt to be first of all a citizen of Sarajevo. Every day he walked through the city unarmed, in order to reassure the people.

His very efforts raised suspicions and in December of 1992 he was arrested on charges of wanting to delay the counteroffensive, thereby damaging the Serbs. He managed to prove the un-soundness of that accusation and thus began the fight against falsehood. He learned to live without the lies of prejudices and ideologies. He wrote to Izetbegović to express his disagreement concerning the military and policemen who plundered houses, apartments and shops owned by Serbs and Croats. He was shocked when paramilitary groups kidnapped people to have them work at the front where they ran the danger of being shot to death.

In 1994 Izetbegović relieved him from his military prerogatives and offered him an honorable pension. But he wrote him a letter in which, among other things, he told him:

"... I spoke of the genocide committed against the Bosnian people. When I was called to testify about the siege of Sarajevo, I spoke of 10,500 people who were killed, including 1,600 children. It did not even cross my mind that members of the Bosnian and Herzegovina army could have committed crimes ... Since the

army and the Government have hidden crimes committed against civilians ... or have not punished them as
they should have, my duty is to distance myself from the
conduct of those who occupy the highest offices of the
State ... As a sign of protest and disagreement, I return
the stars of Brigadier General" (Divjak , 2007, p. 246).

After his resignation Divjak started a new chapter in his life. He
founded an organization that looks after the care of war children
and orphans. With the right formation, a new generation can be
formed, a generation growing up with the concepts of tolerance and
mutual respect. He refused to present himself as the spokesperson
of Sarajevo. He just wants to remain a person doing his duty within
truth and the freedom of a man.

Divjak had the strength to take new actions and be the initiator of
a new beginning because he was acting in an overabundant manner and had sown benefits through his actions. The taking up of
positions, public stances and political or moral acts is the will of the
'*homo agapicus.*' It is not understanding of the spur of the moment,
but action following understanding that characterizes *agape*.

Let us therefore look at it through the different dimensions of agape.
**Intensity**. Divjak is a man of high agapic intensity, because he gives
rise to positive elements and forces. However, his focus is on people
as such. He goes to the house of the Muslim family, he a Serb and
a representative of a conspiring army, taking the risk of being attacked, just to bring about solidarity. But above all, he must decide
when all his points of reference fall apart: the ideology, party and
army, and in his decision he brings about new things which have
the effect of a new birth, a typically agapic one because it breaks the
routine of calculation and convenience in order to follow the 'surplus' that produces benefits. His action is therefore highly intense.
**Extension**. Divjak is universal in defending the multi-ethnicity of
Sarajevo and does not distinguish among Serbs, Croats, Bosnians,
Muslims or Christians. This behavior came at a cost: isolation, mis-
understanding and suspicion to the point of enduring the shame of
betrayal, imprisonment and dismissal, even endangering his very
life. But in order to defeat nationalism, Divjak extended indifference to the merits and demerits of each person to all, i.e. he did not
act out of grudge or interest; he had no recollection and no instrumental project. He knew that only in this way could he safeguard a
piece of humanity in the midst of barbarism, and maintain a multi-

ethnic coexistence in Sarajevo. His extension therefore reached the highest level.

*Duration:* For the General, the end of the universality of Sarajevo turned into the watershed for a new beginning. His agapic action started by saying no to civil war and continued with the civic a plan called: "Instruction builds up Bosnia-Herzegovina," with which he brought together young war victims in order to give them a perspective of peaceful coexistence, one of forgiveness. The commitment led him to the wish that young people be able to question events and find new ideal horizons when faced with dark and unclear situations and do not know in which direction to go without seeking illusions. This is then a long-term commitment which has already started.

*Purity:* Divjak had no other goals than those of maintaining the universality of Sarajevo, which consists of peaceful coexistence between distinct and different people. His unconditional action, not keeping track of dues, overabundant and generative of benefits makes it extremely pure. He went to the home of Muslims, dedicated
himself to the formation of young people in order to spread tolerance and coexistence. His purity level is high.

*Adequacy:* Divjak manifests an adequate agapic way of doing things, i.e. all of his intentions correspond to the actions he undertook. He took a stand, put himself on the line, willingly embarked on political projects in order to oppose the ethnic war in Yugoslavia and to safeguard harmony between the different ethnic groups. He did not tolerate the fact that everything became feasible in the name of Sarajevo's defense; he refused the logic of retaliation, of the recollection of received and inflicted wrongs.

Its effects are coherent with its intentions. He is recognized as a benefactor by the students, by both factions and by the defenseless population. Divjak is a case of *agape* born from the common condition of vulnerability of the human condition, which is expressed in the refusal of making any particular distinction between that given or received and which turns indistinctly to all without memory and without request for any form of payment. Divjak, in finding reasons for deciding, without having any tradition to sustain him, outlined a practice that has shown itself to be critical of that which exists but able, at the same time, of outlining a type of action that formalized a social behavior that was to date unknown.

# 5.4 Conclusion

In this chapter we have seen that *agape* is present in subjects and social movements which are not socially formed by agapic ethics. To us this is the empirical evidence that *agape* is a property of social action and that it is not necessarily linked to a socialization or indoctrination tied to specific social groups. We were also able to see that the context in which it expresses itself often is an extreme context that is characterized by conditions of widespread humiliation, violence and social disownment. Perlasca and Divjak are not persons formed by Christian ethics, nor is the peer-to-peer movement an expression of a religious culture. Their actions, however, break down reciprocity based on calculation and keeping track of what is given and received, thereby expressing a new social fact founded on overabundance, which could be interpreted along the criterion of agapic action. This seems to us to be a crucial element for us to say that *agape* is a research tool. We have also seen that agapic action presents itself with different nuances: of brief duration, such as in Perlasca or in the P2P movement, or intense, as in the case of Divjak and Perlasca; adequate, as in the General of Sarajevo, or inadequate, as in Perlasca and the P2P movement.

# Chapter 6

# Epilogue

Agape certainly is a concept with a theological root. However, it has shown itself heuristically useful to interpret some dimensions of social phenomenology that would not be intelligible without the concept of *agape*. This cultural operation may displease ideologists, be it on the scientist side and on the theological one. The first group may object that a tautological attempt of a religiously oriented sociology is in process, and that therefore there would be no room for the progress of the sociological interpretation. The second group, instead, is horrified when they see *agape* being desecrated, as it is measured, sectioned and broken down in so many aspects that render it profane. Both attitudes tend to avoid, or even more, refuse the construct of *agape* as a sociological interpretative tool, and as a discursive moment of social criticism, capable along this dimension of revealing the violent and uneven nature of social relations.

At the end of our research path, although it not yet an exhaustive one, we seem to be able to say that *agape* is a dimension of reality, which is in front of us and not amenable to negotiate its phenomenal dimension. Be that as it may, rejected or ignored, it is instead something that resists and insists, as a fact that does not accept the fact of being minimized, watered down or hidden, a fact which cannot disappear into prejudiced laziness.

We have seen that *agape* manifests itself in extreme contexts, that its overabundance goes beyond every normality of life, that it makes heroes out of those who live it: Perlasca or Divjak are emblematic cases. But we have also found that in its five dimensions that were analyzed, *agape* is rooted in everyday life: offering acts of kindness, giving up one's seat on the train, letting others go ahead, all present themselves as agapic acts.

Agape is necessary to express the reality that lies beyond justice, the latter being well expressed by political philosophy whose main actor is the State. It is the reality that Boltanki used to describe the state of peace within human relationships. And in order to sketch it out, he had to draw from the Western theological Christian tradition, because there was no other tradition capable of expressing, on the normative level, such a dimension. Our contribution aimed at adding to this endeavor the empirical and interpretative dimension of the concept of *agape*, in addition to re-visiting the formalization of the concept.

We could say that *agape* plays a hermeneutical role: alike Hermes, he too interprets the will of the gods, makes it more comprehensible for men, thus allowing them to transcend and extend their attention towards the divine. The origin of the concept of 'hermeneutics' precisely lies in this interpretation / translation of the divine in human terms. But hermeneutics is not only a transposition – more or less difficult and always interpretative, thus perhaps also arbitrary – of a language into another one. The etymology of 'hermeneutics' does not perhaps go back to 'Hermes' but, further back, to the *'herma,'* i.e. a pile of stones placed to mark boundaries. The god Hermes creates various expressive genres, contributes to culture, therefore gives orders to society, but constantly goes beyond the boundaries that he contributed to creating. Agape and Hermes are then messengers who transcend the boundaries of both worlds, putting in contact the Olympians and humanity, that is – in Platonic terms – the worlds of ideas and of tangible reality, the general and the particular. In other words, hermeneutics is also going beyond already given boundaries. In Hermes this becomes even more evident through his transgressive behavior, which shatters taboos and violates set rules. But this is even more the case for *agape*.

In this sociological transposition, *agape* helps us in the interpretative act of social reality, to delimit and translate, and then leads us in the analysis of social phenomena. This was ultimately the goal that the wise person had set for himself: to simply introduce in the sociological lexicon a tool of analysis for reality; that reality in which one can observe the fact of going beyond set boundaries, to shatter taboos, to go beyond set and codified rules within an arbitrary normality. Because of this, *agape* manifests itself as critical concept. We share the affirmation of Mauro Magatti (1960 - ) for whom from a sociological perspective:

> "*agape* cannot become a norm of social life but amounts
> to an opening point within social order that is able to
> liven up relationships among people and continually
> stimulate their renewal" (Magatti, 2007, p.18).

As underlined by Crespi:

> "love appears to be always the better form of infinite

recognition of the other in his irreducible difference;"
(Crespi, 2004, p. 117).

Its characters allow us to recognize the limit of every form of cultural closure and to penetrate and question from the otherness that produces a displacement from one to the other form of determination, producing along this movement a creativity in which human freedom is manifested. If even the dimension of the political could acquire this agapic dimension, one could reconcile with the dimension of the un-political (Esposito, 1988), meaning that power could be legitimized along its dimension of self-limitation in order to respect the private sphere of ethics, of consumption, etc, offering general regulative criteria capable of generating social solidarity and social rights useful for the pluralist coexistence of the different fields of meaning. In fact, an agapic action contains the awareness that to promote the realization of the other means to work on ones' own self-realization and that the autonomy of the other cannot be promoted without one's own autonomy. The otherness of the other is then a condition for ones' own identity. Along this line, *agape* recognizes in the becoming, in the new and foreign, a frontier that needs to be opened and welcomed. This is the viewpoint of a critical 'radical' ability, according to Boltansky and Thèvenot (1999).

In this perspective of things, *agape* prompts us to reconsider the deepest vocation of social sciences; that is, next to the autonomous perspectives of analysis, the emancipating and humanizing character of their own work must be re-asserted, in the sense that it be capable of identifying and managing the inherent contradictions laying in the various forms of politico-social determinations, and promote a greater awareness of the players. In this perspective the connatural opening of *agape* towards every otherness can take on a privileged point of view that – by showing the mechanisms and contradictions of social formations – acts in such a way that sociology can carry out its scientific task and its critical function, while it orients itself towards the transformation of existing social structures and a better adaptation between institutional forms of life and changeable social practices. In this way sociology can rediscover a critical point of view that, through a hermeneutic exchange, could contribute in a specific manner to the social building of reality itself, in an emancipative direction.

According to this vision, sociology can give a contribution to contemporary society, free from every totalizing temptation or being imbued with illuminist prophetism. Thanks to *agape*, being an interpretative category and, at the same time, critical, we could say with Theodor Adorno (1903-1969) that sociology could tend towards "redemption," understood in the sense of overcoming and of adapting, a continuous and never definitive adaptation of social objectifications to the matters of freedom of subjects (Adorno, 1951/1974).

We have attained a non-secondary result along our research path, when we found a consonance for the theme from classical sociologist of the stature of Sorokin, Simmel and Weber, a dimension definitely ignored by scholars of these giants. Sorokin definitely is the one who explicitly worked on this theme, but he was deemed ideological by his contemporaries and successors, many of whom followers of Parsons who succeeded him at the department of sociology in Harvard, changing the nature and objectives of research. Beyond his numerous reflections and research points on the theme of love, Simmel left us an achievement of sociological knowledge: that love is a motivator of social action, which stands side by side with the selfish and altruistic dimension of society. Weber, finally, is the most surprising of all, because he includes agapic love and its influence on the wider ethical horizons. Out of this he notices the typicality and its dimensions, and makes out of it a comparative tool of analysis within different religious contexts. It is a material full of cues, which supports the dignity of the study path undertaken.

But other people have paid attention to the theme of *agape*, in various ways, not just the classical sociologists, but also contemporary authors such as Axel Honneth, Arpad Szakolczai, Winnicott, Archer or Donati, just to name a few. We have looked at social processes, catching sight of an agapic reality, an often unknown one. In the subject's formation it has been shown how, in the formation of individuality, the breaking of the mother-child symbiosis during the first months of life is linked to the ability of the mother of acting overabundantly and of loving the baby in an agapic way, to go along with his frustration, his omnipotent attacks against the maternal body, to persevere with detachment, but not to abandon him, not to respond to his provocations. The maternal figure must have this attitude despite the fact of finding also herself in conditions of psychological weakness, since a part of herself just recently objectified itself and became another self. However, a non-anguished personality – capable of loving again and of public participation in a reality that could manifest itself as being hostile – can be formed only if it manages to live the separation while still feeling loved by the interiorized presence of a lover. Research carried on by post-psychoanalysis tells us that such an experience transforms the protagonists, that the act of loving and of being loved creates a reality *sui generis*, that it does not leave things the way they were before.

But *agape* has its own dimension and interpretative capacity also at the macro historical-comparative level. We saw this while using Szakolczai's research on the theme of grace, which picks up Weberian research from the side of the Renaissance rather than of the Reformation, in order to interrogate oneself about modernity. Grace has been used by us as an act of *agape* received by a beneficiary. Receiving a benefit of an agapic gesture is experienced by the receiver as a grace, an overflowing and unexpected act of benefit, care and attention. From this point of view, we were able to highlight, along the genealogical reconstruction of grace, its link with the deepest roots of the European West: the Hellenic culture, Judaism and Christianity. Each of these roots expresses a dimension of grace: graciousness-beauty, and the theological grace of Judaism and of Christianity.

During our research, we have able to ascertain that *agape* is present not only at levels of minimal daily social action (as are acts of kindness to strangers), nor only at the level of individual heroes, but it is also found at the macro level. In fact, there is a dimension of the analysis which allows us to glimpse the conditions for the opening of the system of relationships toward a system that rethinks the relationship, that expresses at the same time difference and social unity, but also as a way of thinking about love, a way that is not just elective, as happens in *philia*.

There are life stories which are emblematically agapic, as we have outlined in Perlasca, or with General Jovan Divjak, the protagonist of the resistance of Sarajevo during the time of its siege, but there are also social movements, in addition to long-lasting historical phenomena. Agape expresses an ethical horizon that is well put across by the figure of Sennett's craftsman (2008) that crosses the different eras from antiquity to our days and conveys a presence within the history of *agape*. In fact, the craftsman represents the desire to do something well, concretely for himself, to do a task well for the pleasure it entails. The craftsman is therefore an overabundant subject, which is the typical trait of *agape*.

Similarly to the craftsman, the one who loves is always at risk of failing. The craftsman develops his skill thanks to the constant dialectic between the proper way of doing one thing and the possibility of experiencing errors. The experience of imperfect tools forces the one who uses them to think in terms of repair, beyond the act of creation. The do's and the adjusting are part of a continuum. This is the theme of 'caring for,' which is typical of agapic action (Donati, 2011).

The meaning of the limit, failure, imperfection, of not responding to conflict, of resisting it, of confronting it, but also of accepting it and living it, make of the craftsman a subject capable of building communities. By opening himself to the outside world, the craftsman accepts the fact of having to answer for his actions, and 'creates a community,' in the sense that he selects good practices, sets comprehensible quality parameters, descending to the level of the 'others.' He does not stop at invidious comparison, and does not use competence to humiliate non-experts, but builds a relationship with the otherness.

The craftsman, like the *homo agapicus*, constructs a dialogue between concrete practices and thought. Openness is an effect of experience. The German language splits the idea of experience in two words: *Erlebnis* and *Erfahrung*. The first one indicates an event, an action or a relationship that provokes an impression, an internal emotion. The second one points to an event or a relationship that opens the subject toward what is outside of him. Agape, like the artisan, indicates to us that we should never decouple these two dimensions of practice and of feeling. The difficulties, as well as the possibilities, in doing things well are also applicable to the building of human relationships: people need to train themselves in reciprocal relationships in order to learn and perfect such rapports, to avoid the risk of getting trapped in the thought and action of the means-to-end logic.

In this sense, *agape* presents itself as a craftsman, critical of the instrumental action which is typical of Capitalism and of power. Taking up a suggestion of Hannah Arendt, *agape* tells us that laws should be transitory. In fact, *agape* imagines that rules generated by a deliberative process are put in doubt by changes in conditions and the extent in which subjects subsequently reflect about them. There Arendt brings about a contribution founded on the intuition that the political process is equivalent to the human condition of bringing children to the world, and then letting them go on their own. To describe such a process of birth, training and separation in political life, he uses in fact the term of birth. What is fundamental about life is that we need, at the same time, principles that direct us – potentially strong principles – but also at the same time able to welcome novelty and openness towards what is new. The attempt is precisely to explore, with *agape*, a critical point of view to go against the swirling current of our times, a current made of contractual rules, of loneliness and widespread anxiety. In this sense, in addition to sociology, *agape* presents itself as an ethical horizon and expresses a need for freedom that will never be able to be defined.

# Index

# Bibliography

Adorno T. W., 1971, *Minima Moralia*, Milano, Mondadori; ed. or. 1951.

Allen P. J., (ed.) 1963, *Pitirim A. Sorokin in Review*, Duke University Press, Durham (N.C.)

Archer M., 2006, *La conversazione interiore*, Erickson, Trento; ed. or. 2003.

Arendt H., 1994, *Vita activa. La condizione umana*, Bompiani, Milano; ed. or. 1958.

Aristotele, 1987, *Etica nicomachea*, Rusconi, Milano.

Bauman Z., 2004, *Amore liquido. Sulla fragilita dei legami affettivi*, Laterza, Bari-Roma; ed. or. 2003.

Bellah, R. 1999."Max Weber and World-Denying Love: A Look at the Historical Sociology of Religion."Journal of the American Academy of Religion 67(2):277-304.

Berger P.L., 1999, *Homo Ridens. La dimensione comica dell'esperienza umana*, Il Mulino, Bologna; ed. or. 1997.

Beck U. and Beck E., 1996, *Il normale caos dell'amore*, Bollati Boringhieri, Torino; ed or. 1995.

Bianco A., 2011, *Georg Simmel: le forme dell'amore*, in SMP, vol. 2, n. 4, pp. 51-64.

Blumer H., 1969, *Simbolic Interactionism: Perspective and Method*, Englewood Cliffs, N. J., Prentice Hall.

Boltanski L., 1990, *L'Amour et la Justice comme competences.Trois essais de sociologie de l'action*, Metailie, Paris.

Boltanski L., 2005, *Stati di pace. Una sociologia dell'amore*, Vita e Pensiero, Milano.

Boltanski L., 2009, *De la critique. Precis de sociologie de l'emancipation*, Paris, Gallimard.

Boltanski L. Thevenot L., 1999, *A sociology of critical capacity*, in "European Journal of Social Theory", vol. II, n. 3, pp. 358-77.

Bourdieu P., 2003, *Per una teoria della pratica.Con tre studi di etnologia cabila*, Raffaello Cortina, Milano; ed. or. 1972.

Bourdieu P., 1991, *Lezione sulla lezione*, Marietti, Milano.

Brun J. 1980, *Introduction, in Les Oeuvre de l'amour*, Orante, Paris, pp. XV e XVII.

Bruni L., 2007, *La ferita dell'altro*, Il Margine, Milano.

Bruni L., 2010, *L'ethos del mercato. I fondamenti antropologici e relazionali dell'economia*, Milano, Bruno Mondadori.

Burkert W., 1977, *Griechische Religion der archaischen und klassischen Epoche*, Verlag W. Kohlhammer GmbH, Stuttgart-Berlin-Koln; trad. it., *La religione greca*, Jaka Book, Milano, 2010.

Cacciari M., 2006, *Eros e Agape*, in 'Confronti d'autunno', XV ed., dattiloscritto, Faenza.

Caille A. e Chanial P., 2008, *La Decouverte*, "Revue du Mauss", vol. 2, n. 32, pp. 5-31.

Coda P., 1994, *L'agape come grazie e liberta. Alla radice della teologia e prassi dei cristiani*, Citta Nuova, Roma.

Colasanto M. e Iorio G., 2009, *Sette proposizione sull'Homo Agapicus*, in 'Nuova Umanita', n. 182, pp. 252-278.

Collins R., 2004, *Interaction Ritual Chains*, Princeton University Press, Princeton, N.J.

Crespi F., 2002, *Introduzione alla sociologia*, Bologna, Il Mulino.

Crespi F., Jedloswski P., Rauty R., 2000, *La sociologia. Contesti storici e modelli culturali*, Laterza, Bari-Roma.

Dahme H.J., Rammstedt A., 1984a, Die Aktualitat Georg Simmels, Frankfurt, Suhrkamp.

Dahme H.J., 1984b, *Georg Simmel und die Moderne*, Frankfurt, Suhrkamp.

Deaglio M., 2009, *La banalita del bene*, Milano, Feltrinelli.

Derrida J., 1996, *Donare il tempo. La moneta falsa*, Milano, Raffaello Cortina.

Divjak J., 2007, *Sarajevo mon amour*, Avellino, Infinito.

Durkheim E., 1893, *La divisione del lavoro sociale*, Milano, Comunita; ed. it. 1971.

Eagle M. N., 1993, *La psicoanalisi contemporanea*, Bari-Roma, Laterza.

Eisenstadt S.N., 1986, *The Origins and Diversity of Axial Age Civilisations*, New York, University of New York.

Elias N., 1987, *La societa di corte*, Bologna, Il Mulino.

Elias N., *Il processo di civilizzazione*, Bologna, Il Mulino.

Esposito R., 1988, *Categorie dell'impolitico*, Il Mulino, Bologna.

Foucault, M., 1978, *La volonta di sapere*, Feltrinelli, Milano; ed. or. 1971.

Foucault, M., 1985, *La cura di se*, Milano, Feltrinelli.

Foucault, M., 1996, *Discorso e verita nella Grecia antica*, Roma, Donzelli.

Foucault, M., 1998, *Sorvegliare e punire*, Bologna, Il Mulino.

Gallino L., 1991, *Solidarieta*, in Dizionario di Sociologia, Torino, Utet.

Garfinkel H., 1967, *Studies in Ethnomethodology*, Englewood Cliffs, N. H., Prentice Hall.

Giddens A., 1995, *La trasformazione dell'intimita*, Il Mulino, Bologna; ed. or. 1992.

Good W. J., 1959, *The Theoretical Importance of Love*, "American Sociological Review", vol. 24, n. 1, pp. 38-47.

Gouldner A., 1997, *La sociologia e la vita quotidiana*, a cura e con introduzione di Rauty R., Armando editore, Roma.

Habermas J., 1981, *Teoria dell'agire comunicativo*, 2 vol., Il Mulino, Bologna; ed. or. 1981.

Hazo R. G., 1967, a cura di, *The Idea of Love*, Praeger, New York.

Hegel F., 1971, *Scritti di filosofia del diritto*, Bari, Laterza; ed or. 1802-3.

Hobbes T., 1974, *Leviatano*, 2 voll., Laterza, Roma-Bari; ed. or. 1651.

Hochschild A.R., 2006, Per amore o per denaro. La commercializzazione della vita intima, Il Mulino, Bologna, ed. or. 2003.

Honneth A.,2002, *Lotta per il riconoscimento*, Milano, Il Saggiatore; ed. or 1992.

Honneth A., Iorio G., Campelo F., 2011, *Le condizioni per una sociologia dell'agape*, in 'Sociologia'.

Hillery G. A., 1984, *Gemeinschaft Verstehen: A Theory of the Middle Range*, Social Forces, Vol. 63, N. 2, pp. 307-334.

Iorio G., 2005, *La nascita della sociologia e la relazione sociale*, in 'Nuova Umanita', n. 162, pp. 831-849.

Iorio G., 2011a, *Agape: un concetto per le scienze sociali*, in SMP, vol. 2, n. 3, pp. 101-15.

Iorio G., 2011b, con Campello F., *La sociologia e l'amore come agape*, in SMP, vol. 2, n. 3, pp. 257-262.

Iorio G., 2011c, *L'agire agapico come categoria interpretativa per le scienze sociali*, in 'Sociologia', XLV (3), pp. 37-44.

Johnston B.V., 1996, *Pitirim A. Sorokin: An Intellectual Biography*, University of Kansas Press, Lawrence Kierkegaard S., 1983, Gli atti dell'amore, Rusconi, Milano.

Kuhn T. S., 1962, *La struttura delle rivoluzioni scientifiche*, Einaudi, Torino ed. it. 1978

Levine D., Carter E. B., Gorman E.M., 1976, *Simmel's Influence on American Sociology I*, in "American Journal of Sociology", vol. 81, n. 5, pp. 813-845.

Lonergan B., 1970, *Grazia e liberta: la grazia operante nel pensiero di S. Tommaso*, Universita Gregoriana, Roma.

Luhmann N., 1987, Amore come passione, Laterza, Bari-Roma.

Magatti M., 2005, *Introduzione*, in Boltanski L., op. cit: 7-18.

Marion J. L., 2001, *Dato che. Saggio per una fenomenologia della donazione*, tr. it. di Rosaria Caldarone, a cura di Nicola Reali, Sei, Torino 2001, pp. 399; or. fr. *Etant donne. Essai d'une phenomenologie de la donation*, Puf, Paris 1997, 2 ed. corrigee, Ivi 1998.

Matza D., 1966, "Poverty and Disreputable", in Smelser N.J. e Lipset S., (eds.), *Social Structure and Social Mobility in Economic Growth*, Aldine Press, Chicago.

Mauss M., 1965, *Teoria generale della magia e altri saggi*, Torino, Einaudi; ed or. 1923-24.

Merton R. K., 1949/1959-1971, *Teoria e struttura sociale*, Bologna, Il Mulino.

Nietzsche F., 1985, *La gaia scienza*, Editori Riuniti, Torino; ed. or. 1882.

Nietzsche F., 1986, *Cosi parlo Zarathustra*, CDE, Milano; ed. or. 1886.

Nietzsche F., 1990, *Frammenti postumi*, 1885-1887, 7 [60], in Opere complete, vol. 8/1, a cura di Colli G. e M. Montinari, Milano, Adelphi.

Nissim C. , 2011, *La bonta insensata*, Mondadori, Milano.

Nygren A., 1971, *Eros e agape: la nozione cristiana dell'amore e le sue trasformazioni*, Bologna, Il Mulino.

Parsons T., 1937, *The Structure of Social Action*, McGrow Hill, New York.

Parsons T., 2005, 'La religione nell'America postindustriale: il problema della secolarizzazione', in Bartolini M. e Prandini P., *Cristianesimo e Modernita*, Gentile, Salerno; ed. or. 1974.

Patocka J., *Socrate*, Bompiani, Milano, 2003; ed. or.1947.

Platone, 1993, *Fedro*, Rusconi, Milano.

Platone, 1974, *Opere*, vol. II, Laterza, Bari.

Ricoeur P., 1999, *Le paradigme de la traduction*, in "Esprit", 253, juin, pp. 8-19; trad. it. *Il paradigma della traduzione*, in idem, *La traduzione. Una sfida etica*, Morcelliana, Brescia, 2001.

Rosati M., 2001, *La solidarieta nelle societa complesse*, in *La solidarieta in questione*, Crespi F. e Moscovici S., (a cura di), Roma, Meltemi, pp. 16-81.

Schutz A., 1979, *Saggi sociologici*, Utet, Torino.

Sennett R., 2004, *Rispetto. La dignita umana in un mondo di diseguali*, Il Mulino, Bologna; ed. or. 2003.

Simmel G., 1989, *Sociologia*, Edizioni Comunita, Milano; ed. or. 1908.

Simmel G., 1997, *La socievolezza*, Armando editore, Roma.

Simmel G., 2001, *Filosofia dell'amore*, Roma, Donzelli.

Societa Mutamento Politica, 2011, *L'agire affettivo.Le forme dell'amore nelle scienze sociali*, Vol. 2, n. 4.

Sombart W., 1967, *Il capitalismo moderno*, Comunita, Torino; ed. or. 1902.

Sorokin P. A., 1927, *Social Mobility*, New York, Harper.

Sorokin P. A., 1937-1941, *Social and Cultural Dynamics*, 4 voll., American Book Company, New York.

Sorokin P. A., 1947, *Society, Culture and Personality*, Harper and Brothers, New York.

Sorokin P. A., 1950, *Altruistic Love: A Study of American Good Neighbors and Christian Saints*, Beacon, Boston.

Sorokin P. A., 1963, *A Long Journey*, College and University Press, New Haven.

Sorokin P. A., 2005, *Il potere dell'amore*, Roma, Citta Nuova; ed. or 1954.

Symonds, M., Pudsey, J. 2006. "The Forms of Brotherly Love in Max Weber's Sociology of Religion." Sociological Theory 24(2):133-149.

Sparti D., 2005, *Culture dell'intimita*, in 'Rassegna Italiana di Sociologia, n. 2, pp. 387-400.

Szackolczai A., 2007a, *Sociology, Religion and Grace*, London, Routledge.

Szackolczai A., 2007b, *Il Rinascimento e le rinascite nella storia: verso una sociologia della grazia*, in Studi di Sociologia, n. 2, pp. 123-145.

Thode H., 1993, *Francesco d'Assisi e le origini dell'arte del Rinascimento in Italia*, Roma, Donzelli.

Tenbruck, F. 1980. "The Problem of Thematic Unity in the Works of Max Weber." British Journal of Sociology 31(3):316-51.

Turner, B. 1983. *For Weber: Essay on the Sociology of Fate*. London: Sage.

Turner, C. 1992. *Modernity and Politics in the Work of Max Weber*. London, Routledge.

Voegelin E., 1956, *Order and History, I. Israel and Revelation*, Baton Rouge, Louisiana University Press.

Von Balthaasar H., 1981, *Nuovi punti fermi*, Jaca Book, Milano.

Weber M., 2010, *L'etica protestante e lo spirito del capitalismo*, Milano, Rcs; ed. or. 1904-5.

Weber M., 1920a, "Einleitung" In Gesammelte Aufsutze zur Religionssoziologie vol. 1. Tubingen, J.C.B. Mohr.

Weber M., 1920b, "Zwischenbetrachtung" In Gesammelte Aufsutze zur Religionssoziologie vol. 1. Tubingen, J.C.B. Mohr.

Vozza , 2001, *Introduzione*, in Simmel, op. cit.

Weber M., [1915] 1948a, "The Social Psychology of the World Religions." In From Max Weber, edited and translated by H. H. Gerth and C.W. Mills, London, RKP.

Weber M., [1915] 1948b, "Religious Rejections of the World and Their Directions." In From Max Weber, edited and translated by H. H. Gerth and C. W. Mills, London, RKP.

Weber M., [1906, 1920] 1948c, "The Protestant Sects and the Spirit of Capitalism." In From Max Weber, edited and translated by H. H. Gerth and C. W. Mills, London, RKP.

Weber M., [1915] 1951, *The Religion of China*, New York, Free Press.

Weber M., [1917-1919] 1952, *Ancient Judaism*, New York, Free Press.

Weber M., [1916-1917] 1958, *The Religion of India*, New York, Free Press.

Weber M., [1921] 1978, *Economy and Society*, Berkeley, CA: University of California Press.

Weber M., [1904, 1920] 1985, *The Protestant Ethic and the Spirit of Capitalism*. London, Unwin.

Weber M., [1916-1917] 1996, *Die Wirtschaftsethik der Weltreligionen: Hinduismus und Buddhismus*. Tubingen, J.C.B. Mohr.

Weber M., [1921] 2001, Wirtschaft und Gesellschaft: Religiuse Gemeinschaften. Tubingen, J.C.B. Mohr.

Winnicott D. W., 1970, *Sviluppo affettivo e ambiente. Studi sulla teoria dello sviluppo affettivo*, Armando, Roma.

Winnicott D. W., 1997, *Gioco e realta*, Armando, Roma.

Wittgenstein L., 1964, *Tractatus logico-philosophicus e Quaderni 1914-1916*, Einaudi, Torino; ed. or. 1918.

www.ingramcontent.com/pod-product-compliance
Lightning Source LLC
Chambersburg PA
CBHW061751270326
41928CB00011B/2458